Remembering
September 11, 2001
What We Know Now

Titles in the Issues in Focus Today *series:*

Remembering September 11, 2001

What We Know Now

ISSUES IN FOCUS TODAY

Mara Miller

 Enslow Publishers, Inc.
40 Industrial Road
Box 398
Berkeley Heights, NJ 07922
USA

http://www.enslow.com

Library of Congress Cataloging-in-Publication Data

Miller, Mara, 1968-
     Remembering September 11, 2001 : what we know now / Mara Miller.
        p. cm. — (Issues in focus today)
     Summary: "Examines the terrorist attacks on September 11, 2001, including the events that led to the attack; the attack on the World Trade Center Towers, the Pentagon, and United Flight 93; and the aftermath of the attacks"—Provided by publisher.
     Includes bibliographical references and index.
     ISBN-13: 978-0-7660-2931-6
     ISBN-10: 0-7660-2931-X
     1. September 11 Terrorist Attacks, 2001—Juvenile literature. 2. Terrorism—United States—Juvenile literature. I. Title.
     HV6432.7.M55 2010
     973.931—dc22
                                    2009006508

Printed in the United States of America

052010 Lake Book Manufacturing, Inc., Melrose Park, IL

10 9 8 7 6 5 4 3 2 1

Illustration Credits: Associated Press, pp. 5, 7, 15, 17, 24, 29, 37, 40, 42, 46, 48, 50, 51, 54, 71, 75, 79, 84, 86, 91, 93, 95, 97, 99, 101, 105; Andrea Booher/FEMA News Photo, pp. 5, 62; Chao Soi Cheong/Associated Press, pp. 3, 5, 32; Ron Haviv/Associated Press, pp. 57, 59; James Nachtwey/Associated Press, pp. 5, 43; Michael Rieger/FEMA News Photo, pp. 66, 103; Gulnara Samoilova/Associated Press, p. 35; James Toutellotte/U.S. Customs and Border Protection, p. 77.

Cover Illustrations: U.S. Navy photo by Jim Watson/Associated Press. (Shown are the remains of the World Trade Center, photographed on September 13, 2001.)

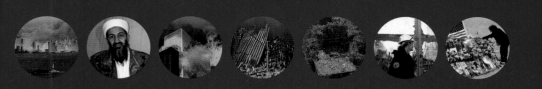

C o n t e n t s

Dedication

*There are too many names to list in my dedication—almost
three thousand, plus their friends and families. The term
"victims" does not describe the loss of these individuals. Through
my research, I have learned about some of the people who died
in the attacks on 9/11. They lived full lives, loved, and were
loved by others. I doubt that I would have met many of them if
they had lived, but I would have liked to. I dedicate this book
to all those who died in the attack and to all of us living who
have been injured by the tragedy.*

Acknowledgments

*A special thanks to Dan Byman, Director of the Center
for Peace and Security Studies at Georgetown University,
for helping me get it right.*

It was 8:14 in the morning of September 11, 2001. Skies in the eastern states were clear and blue. The day was bright. Visibility was perfect. Weather conditions for flying did not get much better.

Air traffic controller Pete Zalewski told American Airlines Flight 11 to "climb and maintain flight level three-five-zero, 35,000 feet."[1] Zalewski worked at Boston Air Traffic Control Center. He and the other air traffic controllers were responsible for the planes going in and out of Logan International Airport. They made sure the planes had plenty of space and avoided collision.

There was no reply from Flight 11, and the plane stayed at the altitude of 29,000 feet. Zalewski wondered why the pilots were not responding, but he was not too concerned. Perhaps the pilots were not paying attention or there was a problem with the radio's frequency.

"Are you listening?" he asked.[2] The pilots did not answer. Then the plane veered northwest, and the transponder shut off.

A plane's transponder tracks the flight's number, position, speed, and altitude for the air traffic controllers. Without it, a plane becomes a blip on the radar screen that only shows the speed. Zalewski thought something might be seriously wrong. But he was not thinking hijacking. The plane turned south.

Then, Zalewski heard a foreign voice through the transmitter. "We have some planes," it said.[3] Zalewski did not understand this first announcement. It was too garbled. However, the next ones gave him chills. "Nobody move. Everything will be okay. If you try to make any moves, you'll endanger yourself and the airplane. Just stay quiet."[4] It was now clear that American Airlines Flight 11 had been hijacked. "I felt from those voices the terror. For some reason, I knew something seemed worse than just a normal hijack. It just seemed very different to me," he later recalled.[5]

Zalewski yelled to his supervisor, "Get over here immediately—right now!"[6] He put the transmissions on speaker so that others could hear. An assistant came to help listen. It was the first hijacking on a U.S. airline in more than a decade. Air traffic controllers began to scramble. They tried to guess the plane's destination. Previously hijacked flights had landed at airports where the hijackers would try to negotiate for something. The controllers thought maybe the plane was heading for New York's John F. Kennedy Airport or Cuba.[7] They played back the recorded transmissions as they tried to figure out what was happening with the plane.

Boston Center managers alerted their superiors of the

hijacking. They also contacted the military through the Cape Cod facility of the Federal Aviation Administration (FAA). The FAA reached the Northeast Air Defense Sector (NEADS) at 8:37 A.M.

"We have a problem here. We have a hijacked aircraft headed towards New York, and we need you guys to, we need someone to scramble some F-16s or something up there, help us out."

"Is this real-world or exercise?" the person at NEADS asked.

"No, this is not an exercise—not a test," the FAA confirmed.[8]

Flight 11 entered controller John Hartling's airspace. Another plane was nearby. He asked the pilots of United Flight 175 if they could see the American Airlines jet. The pilots said that Flight 11 was still at about 28,000–29,000 feet. Hartling then asked United 175 to turn 30 degrees to the right. He wanted to keep them out of Flight 11's path.[9] What Hartling did not know was that United 175 also had terrorists on board and would be the next plane in trouble.

Hartling watched Flight 11's speed slow rapidly. Without the transponder, it was the only indication he had that the plane was descending. The plane descended below where the radar could track it. The blip disappeared from the screen.

Seconds after, another air traffic controller, Dave Bottiglia, realized that United Flight 175's transponder signal was also gone.

In the Plane

Flight attendants on board Flight 11 called the airline to let them know that they were in trouble. At about 8:20 A.M., Betty Ong reached the American Airlines reservation desk. She told a reservationist that "the cockpit's not answering. Somebody's stabbed in business class and ... I think there's mace ... that we can't breathe. I don't know, I think we're getting hijacked."[10]

She also reported that the purser and galley flight attendant had been stabbed. She said that the plane was flying erratically.

Another flight attendant, Madeline "Amy" Sweeney, was sitting next to Ong in the back of the plane. The two women were determined to give as much information as they could to the people on the ground. Sweeney called the American Airlines Flight Services Office and was connected to Michael Woodward. She reported the stabbings of the flight attendants in first class and also of a passenger. She gave the seat numbers of some of the hijackers so that officials would know who they were.

It is impossible to know exactly how the hijacking occurred on board the plane. Based on the phone calls, transmissions, and seat records, it is believed that at approximately 8:14 A.M. at least two of the five hijackers seated in business class forced their way into the cockpit. They may have jammed their way in or lured the pilots out with the stabbings. It is also possible that they attacked the flight attendants in order to get the keys to the cockpit door. The hijackers sprayed some type of mace or pepper spray into the cabin that made it difficult to breathe. This forced the other first-class passengers into the back of the plane. The hijackers claimed to have a bomb.

At 8:44 A.M., about a half hour after the hijacking started, Sweeney told Woodward, "Something is wrong. We are in a rapid descent … are all over the place."[11] Woodward asked Sweeney to look out the window to see if she could determine where they were.

"We are flying very, very low. We are flying way too low," she said. "Oh my God we are way too low."[12] The phone call abruptly ended.

Inside the North Tower

At 8:46 A.M., Flight 11 with eighty-one passengers (including the terrorists), nine flight attendants, and two pilots ripped into the World Trade Center's North Tower. The Boeing 767 went in at an angle, traveling at approximately 470 miles per hour. From wing tip to wing tip, it cut a path from the 93rd to the 99th floor. The main body of the plane left a hole four stories high. The impact severely damaged the supporting columns. The walls of the escape staircases collapsed, making them impassable. Pipes that fed the fire sprinkler system were severed. Around 10,000 gallons of jet fuel ignited.[13] A fireball burst out through the gaping hole. The resulting explosion shook the building's core.

The tower was designed to be flexible to cope with high winds. It recoiled from the impact, causing the upper floors to sway. Black smoke poured from the gaping hole and blown-out windows.

Many inside the building felt the explosion and thought that a bomb had gone off. The World Trade Center had withstood a bomb explosion in 1993.

Before 9/11, a plane flying into a building was almost unimaginable. But Ezra Aviles saw the plane as it hit. He was looking out his window on the 61st floor. "It seems to be an American Airlines jetliner came in from the northern direction, toward—from the Empire State Building, toward us," he said in a voice mail to the Port Authority. "… Don't come near the building if you're outside. Pieces are coming down."[14]

People above the impact were trapped. The emergency stairwells were destroyed or blocked by debris.

On the 106th floor, a breakfast conference was about to begin when the plane struck. The floor featured an observation deck known as the "Top of the World" and an elegant restaurant called Windows on the World. A normal fire would have been contained to the floor where it started. Each floor was designed to act as a fire-tight compartment. But this fire was so intense that seven floors above the impact, the rooms began to fill with smoke.

Frantic calls and e-mails went out to loved ones. "Mom, I'm not calling to chat," Garth Feeney told his mother from the 106th floor. "I'm in the World Trade Center and it's been hit by a plane.... There are 70 of us in one room. They have closed the doors and they are trying to keep the smoke out."[15]

Restaurant manager Doris Eng and assistant general manager Christine Olender tried to direct the 170 guests and employees to safety, but there was little they could do. "The stairways are full of smoke," Olender reported to Port Authority officer Steve Maggett. "And my ... and my electric ... my fire phones are out."[16]

Maggett told Olender that "everyone" in the fire department was on their way.

"The condition up on 106 is getting worse," she repeated the urgency of the situation.

"We are doing our best to get up to you right now," he tried to reassure her.[17] But Maggett did not know that the crash had cut off access to the upper floors. Nor did he know that the time for rescues was extremely limited.

On the 104th floor, about fifty people who were working at Cantor Fitzgerald, a financial services company, crammed into a corner office to avoid the smoke. Andrew Rosenblum, a stock trader and vice president in the company, called his wife. He gave her the names and phone numbers of the people near him. He asked her to call their spouses. He told her they had used a computer terminal to break through a window to get some air.[18]

The 91st floor was the first level beneath the impact to have a passable exit.

Mike McQuaid had been installing fire extinguishers for new tenants when he heard the explosion. He made his way to the only surviving stairway with some of his crew. No one was coming down from above. The stairway was dark. Sheetrock was blown off the walls. The steel behind it now showed. The way up looked completely blocked.[19] McQuaid began his ninety-one-floor descent. As he went down, he met many others from lower floors making their way out. The descent was slow but orderly.

On the 86th floor, well below the impact, Patricia Puma and James Gartenberg found themselves trapped by collapsed walls and debris. "The explosion … seemed to come from the inside out, rather than the outside in," Gartenberg told a *New York Times* reporter by phone while stuck in the tower. "The fire door is blocked…. The elevators are completely blown out."

"It looked like the explosion came up through the elevator," Puma reported.[20]

Fireballs had in fact blasted down elevator shafts, blowing out elevator doors and shaft walls.

Harry Waizer was in one of the elevators when the plane hit. "There was an explosion. The elevator started to shake," Waizer recalled. "Then it started to plummet and burst into flames."[21] Waizer was badly burned, but he survived. On other elevators, people found themselves trapped.

Calls flooded 911 emergency lines. More than three thousand emergency calls came in the first eighteen minutes alone.[22] The operators did their best to be professional and calming in a time of crisis when all their phone lines were blinking. With very limited outside information, operators gave the advice they knew for a high-rise fire. They recorded where the people were and told those inside to wait for the rescuers who were on their way. For those on the floors above the impact, waiting was the only thing they could do.

On the Ground

Jules Naudet was filming Fire Chief Joseph Pfeifer for a documentary when the Boeing 767 screamed overhead. He turned his camera just in time to catch the plane slamming into the building. The audio caught the shouts of astonishment. New Yorkers heard the explosion and looked up to see a column of smoke rising from the North Tower. Most people in the United States were unfamiliar with terrorism. Most thought the crash had to be an accident. But Chief Pfeifer noted that it "looked like a direct attack."[23]

Pfeifer immediately radioed in the first report and transmitted a second alarm. He told the units he was with to head to the World Trade Center. Then he transmitted a third alarm. Each alarm call sends more firefighters to the scene. He arrived at the towers four minutes after the plane hit.

Fire chiefs at the scene quickly realized that they would not be able to put the fire out. This would be a rescue mission. They called in a fifth alarm, the highest level, to get more help. Sirens blared as emergency workers rushed to the scene.

Within ten minutes, the deputy fire safety director called for a full evacuation of the complex. A full evacuation is difficult and has risks of injury, especially for the disabled or people in poor health. It had never been practiced at the World Trade Center as a drill. It was always assumed that a fire could be contained to the floor where it started.

Not everybody heard the call to evacuate. The public address systems were damaged, and the orders were not relayed to 911 operators or the fire department dispatchers. In general, getting and dispensing information were problems for the fire department. Fire chiefs did not know which floors were hit, how fast the fire was spreading, which stairways were passable, or whether water was available on upper floors.

The radio systems that firefighters used worked poorly in high-rise situations. A repeater (a device that helps boost and relay radio signals) had been installed in the World Trade Center prior to 9/11 to help solve this problem. But on 9/11, the repeater only partially worked. Communication problems made coordinating the rescue difficult.

Chief Pfeifer checked for elevator service inside the building. It appeared that all ninety-nine elevators in the North

"We have a number of floors on fire here.... Transmit a third alarm."

FDNY Battalion Chief Joseph Pfeifer, reporting on the first plane crash at the World Trade Center

BUNKER COAT AND HELMET
worn by FDNY Battalion Chief
the first fire chief to arrive at th
Center on September 11
Coat gift of the Fire Departme
City of New York
Helmet lent by Joseph W. Pt

RESCUE TOOL
recovered with the body
a New York City firefigh
collapse of the World T
Gift of Joseph W. Pfeife

...ne of the first fire-and-rescue units to arrive at the
...rade Center was Engine 7, Ladder 1, led by Battalion Chief
...feifer. While on a routine call nearby, Pfeifer had seen the
... hit. He set up a command center in the lobby of the
...r and sent firefighters upstairs to begin rescue work.

...uth tower collapsed, sending blinding clouds of smoke
...the north tower, Pfeifer radioed his men to evacuate
...oon afterward, the north tower collapsed.

...adder 1 survived, but hundreds of other firefighters
...ding the chief's brother, Lt. Kevin Pfeifer.

FDNY Lt. Kevin Pfeifer, photographed outside
Engine Co. 33 on September 8, 2001

The coat and helmet worn by NYFD Battalion Chief Joseph Pfeifer are on display at a commemorative exhibit. Pfeifer was the first fire chief to arrive at the World Trade Center after the first plane hit.

Tower were out. Without elevators, firefighters had to climb the stairs laden with fire protective suits and heavy equipment. The basic load of just their suit, boots, helmet, oxygen tank, and mask weighed more than fifty pounds.

As the firefighters went up, they passed scores of people making their way down.

The stairways in the World Trade Center were not built for a full evacuation, and they were not wide enough to accommodate all the people. They were crowded with people trying to get out. But people made way for the rescuers to get through.

In the lobby, firefighters directed the people coming out of the stairways. Flaming debris was falling from the building. It was too dangerous to exit through the main doors. People were directed out through the Marriott Hotel restaurant between the towers or a shopping concourse that ran beneath the buildings.[24]

The police department's Emergency Services Unit (ESU) also responded within five minutes of the strike. They set up a command post a few blocks away from the World Trade Center. The ESU was specially trained to help in situations where people were trapped by fire. Police Chief Joseph Esposito radioed a request for a level-4 mobilization. It was the department's highest state of alert. It would bring about a thousand officers to the scene.

Most of the police officers helped control the situation outside the buildings. They directed traffic and people away from the World Trade Center. They helped the people evacuate the buildings. Members of the specially trained ESU team went to help the fire department inside the burning tower.

The Media

Around the country, people were just getting up and starting their day when they heard the news. Major television stations began broadcasting live reports within six minutes of the strike.

United Flight 175 hit the South Tower of the World Trade Center at 9:03 A.M.

But they did not have a lot of information. "We understand that a plane has crashed into the World Trade Center," CBS anchor Bryant Gumbel reported. "We don't know anything more than that. We don't know if it was a commercial aircraft. We don't know if it was a private aircraft. We have no idea how many were on board or what the extent of the injuries are."[25]

Many reporters, photographers, and cameramen hurried to the scene to gather more information. Gumbel spoke live with eyewitnesses. Cameras zoomed in on the smoke billowing from the upper floors of the North Tower.

At 9:02 A.M., Gumbel was speaking to Theresa Renaud, who was in a nearby building. Her window looked directly at the World Trade Center. She was describing the original explosion when the second plane, United 175, flew into the South Tower.

"Oh, there's another one—another plane just hit," Renaud exclaimed live on the air. "Oh, my God! Another plane has just hit—it hit another building, flew right into the middle of it.... That was definitely ... on purpose."[26]

This time the nation witnessed the attack. It was not an accident. It was an act of terror. And the terror was just beginning.

At this point, nobody knew for certain who was behind the attack. But terrorism experts already had suspects in mind—Osama bin Laden and the terrorist group Al Qaeda. Al Qaeda was responsible for bombing two U.S. embassies in Africa and the naval ship U.S.S. *Cole*. National Security Advisor Condoleezza Rice recalled a meeting in the afternoon of 9/11 in which they discussed who may have done it. "Everybody assumed that it was Al Qaeda, because the operation looked like Al Qaeda, quacked like Al Qaeda, seemed like Al Qaeda.... I don't think there was ever a doubt in anyone's mind, because we knew enough about the organization to know that this is exactly the kind of thing they would try to do."[27]

It would later be confirmed that Al Qaeda was responsible for the attack on 9/11. But at this point, most people were wondering how anyone could do this and why.

Osama bin Laden and the   2
Threat of AL Qaeda

In August 1996, Osama bin Laden issued a fatwa (a formal religious decree) declaring war against the United States. Among other complaints, he condemned the United States for having troops in Saudi Arabia. Saudi Arabia is home to the two holiest places in Islam—Mecca and Medina. Bin Laden viewed the U.S. presence there as the greatest aggression "incurred by the Muslims since the death of the Prophet [Muhammad]."[1] Bin Laden also railed against the U.S. support of Israel in the conflict between Israel and the Palestinians.

It seemed strange for a man not associated with a country to declare war on a superpower. Most Americans did not know who Osama bin Laden was in 1996. But the threat was not dismissed. Bin Laden's name was known to the Central Intelligence Agency (CIA). Agents had been gathering information about him since 1993. Concerns over his activities led the CIA to form the Bin Laden Unit. This group of about twelve officers studied the reports linked to bin Laden. They tried to form a picture of his activities and disrupt his operations.

At first, the agents thought bin Laden was a financier of terror. They thought he paid for the training and weapons. But by 1996, they knew he played a larger role. They had information that he was the leader of a radical Islamic group called Al Qaeda. They soon learned that Al Qaeda had plans to attack U.S. interests worldwide.

Osama Bin Laden's Early Years

Osama bin Laden grew up rich and religious in Saudi Arabia. His father, Muhammed bin Laden, was a self-made billionaire. He owned the Bin Laden Construction Company. The company built roads, tunnels, power plants, and palaces for the king of Saudi Arabia. Muhammed bin Laden was also trusted with the repairs and expansions of the three holiest mosques in the Islamic religion. These are the mosques in Mecca, Medina, and Jerusalem. As a youth, Osama spent time in these holy shrines. He was proud of his father's involvement. "Because of God's graciousness, [my father] sometimes prayed in all three mosques in one single day," bin Laden told reporters.[2]

Muhammed bin Laden had many wives and many children. He was a strict disciplinarian and a firm believer in Islam. He raised his sons to be the same. Even at a young age, Osama bin Laden seemed more religious than his siblings.

Muhammed bin Laden expected his sons to help in his construction business. "I started working with my father when I was a child," Osama bin Laden said in a 1997 interview. He said he had worked on the expansion of the mosque in Jerusalem. There he "received training in the use of explosives for construction work and [the] demolition of mountains."[3] Muhammed bin Laden died in a plane crash when Osama was ten years old.

In college, Osama bin Laden's ideas of Islam became more radical. He studied the writing of Sayyid Qutb, who condemned the United States for its greed, personal freedoms, economic system, racism, sports, music, clothes, and even haircuts.[4] Qutb rejected Western ways as ungodly. He encouraged Muslims to actively fight against barbarism, decadence, and disbelief. It was a condition he called *jahiliyya*—an ignorance of God's guidance. Muslims use the term to refer to the spiritual state of Arab lands before the revelation of Islam. For Qutb, the struggle was between God and Satan. Muslims who disagreed with his ideas were not real Muslims, he claimed; they were nonbelievers. Therefore they deserved no respect and could even be killed.[5]

Most Muslims do not follow Qutb's stark views. As President George W. Bush noted, "Islam is a faith that brings comfort to a billion people around the world.... It's a faith based upon love, not hate."[6] But Osama bin Laden was deeply influenced by Qutb. He would later use his ideas to justify mass murder, first in Africa and then in the United States. But it was the Soviet-Afghan war that set bin Laden on the road to terrorism. That war cemented bin Laden's beliefs and became a training ground for Islamic extremists.

The Soviet-Afghan War

On December 24, 1979, Soviet transport planes landed in Kabul, the capital of Afghanistan. The planes were loaded with soldiers. The next morning, the Soviets laid floating bridges across the Amu Darya River on Afghanistan's border. Soon after, Soviet tanks rolled across the bridges and into the country. Explosions took out Afghanistan's communication system two days later. Then, as darkness fell, more than seven hundred Soviet agents stormed the Kabul palace. Their mission was to kill the Afghan president. After a bloody battle, they succeeded.

The Soviet Union was a Communist country in Eastern Europe made up of Russia and fourteen other Soviet states. It was a superpower that had conquered many of its Soviet states during World War II. In theory, the government controlled the economy so that goods could be shared equally among the people. Soviet Communism was at odds with the U.S. democracy and its free economy. The Soviet Union also promoted atheism, or disbelief in God.

Afghanistan is an Islamic country. Many Muslims felt that the Soviet invasion of Afghanistan was an attack on Islam. They feared the spread of atheism. For Muslims, this made Afghanistan's fight a holy war, or jihad.

Some Arabs left their countries to fight in Afghanistan. Osama bin Laden, young and religious, made his first trip just weeks after the invasion. He made several more trips during the ten-year war. He brought bulldozers, loaders, dump trucks, and machinery to help build roads and tunnels for the Afghan fighters. He set up guest houses for Muslims drawn to the jihad. He met other Muslims with similar beliefs to his own. Some of the men were members of terrorist organizations in other countries.

The Soviet invasion also angered the United States. At the time, the United States and Soviet Union were enemies. The United States worried about the spread of the Soviet political system, Communism. They also worried that the fall of Afghanistan would give the Soviet Union more power in the Indian Ocean. Therefore, the United States secretly gave money and weapons to groups fighting against the Soviet Union. The money was funneled through Pakistan. There is no evidence that any U.S. money went directly to Osama bin Laden.[7]

More than a million Afghans died during the war. But in the end, the Soviet Union was forced to withdraw. It was an Afghan victory and the defeat of a superpower. The Soviet Union left Afghanistan in 1989. The United States no longer had an interest in the region and stopped sending money.

The war had also destroyed Afghanistan's government. The region has many tribes and ethnic groups. Disagreements surfaced among these groups, and they began fighting against each other. The country spiraled into civil war.

The actual impact the Arab fighters had on the Soviet withdrawal is considered minimal. However, the Arab fighters claimed victory for Islam. "The glory and myth of the superpower was destroyed not only in my mind but also in [the minds of] all Muslims," Osama bin Laden said later.[8]

The Arab fighters returned to their home countries. But they still wanted to fight. Bin Laden did not want the jihadist movement to end either. Bin Laden decided to build an army of devout Muslim men that would respond to the call of jihad anywhere in the world. He formed the group Al Qaeda. Al Qaeda means "the base."

The Rise of Al Qaeda

Osama bin Laden returned to Saudi Arabia well known. Many considered him a hero. But his radical ideas concerned those in power. He was openly critical of the Saudi royal family. He condemned their decision to call on U.S. troops to fight Saddam Hussein's invasion of Kuwait in 1990. The Saudis marked bin Laden's passport and tried to restrict his ability to travel. But bin Laden used his business connections and moved to Sudan in 1991.

In Sudan, bin Laden inspired and financed terrorist activity. He set up businesses and training camps. He began a network of terrorist organizations. Most terror groups focused on specific struggles in Islamic regions. But bin Laden concentrated his efforts on striking the "far enemy"—the United States.

In 1996, bin Laden left Sudan for several reasons. The

Afghan guerrillas pose with an unexploded Soviet bomb in 1981. More than a million Afghans died in the war, but the Soviet Union eventually withdrew its troops.

United States was pressuring Sudan's government to stop sponsoring terrorism. He was a target for assassination. Two attempts had failed in 1994. And the Saudi government continued to act against him by freezing his bank accounts, issuing an arrest warrant, and finally revoking his citizenship.[9]

Bin Laden returned to Afghanistan. The Taliban was in power. The Taliban had stopped much of the civil war, but at a great price to personal freedom. There was no religious freedom. The Taliban forbade women to go to school. Women had to wear burqas that covered them from head to toe; not even their faces showed. Men had to grow beards like the Islamic prophet, Muhammad. No one could be on the street after 9:00 P.M. Playing games, listening to music, and watching TV were forbidden and punishable. The punishments for crimes included amputations, lashings, and stoning.

Bin Laden and the Taliban shared many of the same extremist views. They formed an alliance. Bin Laden helped the Taliban with money and the use of Al Qaeda fighters. In return, the Taliban protected bin Laden. They allowed him to run his terrorist training camps, import weapons, and plan terrorist attacks without interference. An estimated ten thousand to twenty thousand fighters went through training at bin Laden's camps between 1996 and September 11, 2001.[10]

Bin Laden ran Al Qaeda like a business. Decisions about overall policy were made by bin Laden and his closest advisers. Those plans were told to the appropriate people at the next level. The lowest members on the chain would only learn about plans as necessary.

On February 22, 1998, bin Laden issued another fatwa. He announced the formation of World Islamic Front for Jihad against Jews and the Crusaders. The Crusaders were European Christians who tried to retake the Holy Land from the Muslims in the eleventh, twelfth, and thirteenth centuries. Bin Laden considered modern-day and American Christians in this group

The Rise of the Taliban

Years of war and lawlessness made the Afghans desperate. Millions had fled the country. Thousands lived in refugee camps. Many did not have enough food to eat or water to drink. Five to seven million unexploded land mines marred the countryside.[11] Every year, thousands of people were injured when the mines were set off accidentally. Bandits regularly robbed, hijacked, or killed travelers on the roads. Women and children were at risk of being kidnapped and raped.

Islamic schools known as *madrassahs* trained young Afghans in the refugee camps of neighboring Pakistan. Mohummad Omar was a leader in one of these schools. He had fought the Soviets in the Afghanistan War and lost an eye in an explosion. In 1994, he and a group of his followers began fighting the lawlessness on the roads in Afghanistan. They called themselves Taliban, which means "those who seek God."[12]

The Taliban gained support from Pakistan when they reportedly rescued a Pakistani truck convoy from an Afghan warlord. The Taliban freed the convoy and chased the hijacker into the desert. There they shot the man and hung his body from the barrel of a tank as a warning.[13]

By 1996, the Taliban controlled most of Afghanistan. They established order. But with the order came a strict form of Islamic law that ignored many basic human rights.

as well. He called for Muslims "to abide by Allah's order by killing Americans and stealing their money anywhere, anytime, and whenever possible."[14] Bin Laden's words foreshadowed his planned attacks on two U.S. embassies in Africa.

The Attack on U.S. Embassies

On Friday, August 7, 1998, Mohammed Rashed al-'Owhali and a young Saudi named Azzam drove a Nissan truck toward the U.S. embassy in Nairobi, Kenya. The truck contained a bomb weighing several hundred pounds. The men chanted religious poems as they drove.[15] They tried to keep their courage up. They were supposed to die when the bomb exploded.

Al-'Owhali and Azzam believed that their deaths would make them martyrs for Islam. They believed that martyrs gained immediate entrance to paradise when they died.

At the embassy, al-'Owhali jumped out of the truck. He tossed handmade stun grenades and shouted at the guards to open the gate. But the gates remained closed. Meanwhile, Azzam moved the truck closer to the embassy. Al-'Owahali saw that the truck was close enough to complete the mission. He decided that staying when the bomb exploded was an act of suicide, not martyrdom. So he ran away.

The bomb exploded. Embassy walls crumbled. Ceilings collapsed. Glass, smoke, and dust filled the air. A five-story secretarial school next door was completely destroyed.

Susan Mutisya was standing across the street from the embassy when the bomb exploded. "I just started running when I saw the flying glass and concrete hitting people, and the cars catching on fire.... Somehow I managed to get away."[16]

Frank Pressley was inside the embassy. First he heard the popping of the stun grenades. Then there was a huge blast. Pressley was hurled across the room. The force of the explosion "picked me up and I just went . . . flying through the air. . . . I hit the wall," he testified later. Afterward he could not believe what he saw. Walls were missing. Bodies were strewn around. Blood was everywhere. Part of Pressley's jaw was gone.[17]

Nine minutes later, another bomb went off approximately 450 miles away. This bomb exploded in front of the U.S. embassy in Tanzania. Witnesses described a low rumbling like a thunderstorm. Then there was an explosion that rocked the building. "It just went pitch black. There was ... a strange smell, kind of an oily, gritty feeling in the air," recalled Elizabeth Slater. When things cleared, "I was looking at the sky." The walls had fallen on top of her. She was trapped beneath the rubble.[18]

The two bombings killed 224 people, including twelve Americans, and injured more than five thousand. It was a "very well-coordinated, very well-planned attack—clearly not the work of amateurs," said P. J. Crowley, a U.S. government spokesman.[19]

The terrorist al-'Owhali checked into a hospital for minor injuries. He was arrested for having improper identification papers. Under questioning, he confessed to his part in the bombings. He told the investigators about the role of Al Qaeda.

In response, President Bill Clinton ordered a cruise missile attack. The targets were training camps in Afghanistan and a possible chemical weapons laboratory in Sudan that was believed to have ties to Al Qaeda. But terrorist camps are easily rebuilt. The laboratory turned out to make medicine. Many critics argued that it did not have links to chemical weapons. Whether it did or did not was never proven. Regardless, the U.S. response had little impact.

The U.S.S. *Cole*

On October 12, 2000, the U.S.S. *Cole* was refueling in Yemen. It was a huge warship. It carried more than three hundred crew members. The hull was made of reinforced steel.

Also in the harbor was a small fishing boat. The boat contained five hundred to seven hundred pounds of explosives.[20] Two men got in it and sped toward the warship. As they neared the *Cole*, they stood up and waved. Then they detonated the bomb.

The explosion blew a forty-foot-by-sixty-foot hole in the side of the ship.[21] The blast lifted the floor of the crew's dining area and pressed it to the ceiling. Windows were shattered. Water flooded into one of the two engine rooms.[22] Seventeen American sailors died. Thirty-nine were injured.

Officer Christopher Byrnes described the damage on the inside: "It looked like somebody took a giant fork and turned it around like you do spaghetti—just all messed up," he said.[23]

Again the evidence pointed to Al Qaeda. The Yemeni

The Navy destroyer U.S.S. *Cole* is towed from Aden, Yemen, after it was bombed by Al Qaeda in 2000.

government arrested about a half dozen men directly involved in the attack. Shortly after the attack, the presidency changed in the United States. Neither President Clinton nor President Bush took military action against Al Qaeda for the *Cole* bombing.

Americans were outraged at the attacks on the *Cole* and the African embassies. But they seemed far way. The next big attack would hit the United States at home.

The "Planes Operation"

Khalid Sheikh Mohammed wanted to see the World Trade Center crumble. He had played a small role in the 1993 attack.

In that attack, terrorists parked a truck bomb in the World Trade Center's underground garage. The resulting explosion left a hole seven stories high. Six people died. But the towers still stood.

Mohammed began planning for a second chance to destroy the buildings. The truck bomb had not been big enough to bring the buildings down. He needed a new approach. He thought about using aircraft as weapons.[24]

In 1999, Mohammed met with bin Laden in Afghanistan. The men talked about a "planes operation" and developed a list of targets.

Bin Laden chose Mohamed Atta, Ramzi Binalshibh, Marwan al-Shehhi, and Ziad Jarrah to pilot the suicide planes. He chose Atta to lead the operation. The four men had been living in Germany. They had the same anti-American zeal as other Al Qaeda members. But they could speak English and were less likely to stand out in Western culture.

The four men received training in Afghanistan then enrolled in U.S. flight schools. Binalshibh could not get a U.S. visa to enter the country, so Hani Hanjour took his place.

Bin Laden also chose the men who served as the muscle hijackers—the ones who would supply the physical force when they took over the planes. They were taught how to conduct hijackings, disarm air marshals, and handle explosives. They practiced storming the cockpit. They lifted weights and learned basic English phrases. They even butchered sheep so they would know how to use the knives as weapons during the attack.[25]

The hijackers were asked to swear loyalty for a suicide mission. But they were given very few details. Khalid Sheikh Mohammed then told them to get "clean" passports from their home countries before applying for U.S. visas. The passports were likely doctored so that they did not show where the men had traveled.

One Was Stopped

Only one hijacker, Mohamed al Katani, was stopped from entering the United States. Katani was referred to Jose Melendez-Perez because his papers were not filled out correctly. An employee of the Immigration and Naturalization Service (INS) in Orlando, Melendez-Perez was a seasoned officer with experience observing body language and detecting fraud. He asked Katani questions. Katani was arrogant and aggressive. He gave Melendez-Perez the creeps. Something was not right. Katani did not have a return ticket or hotel reservation. He said he did not know where he was going in the United States. He did not have a credit card or enough money. First he said someone was picking him up and then changed his story. When placed under oath, Katani refused to answer the questions.[26]

Melendez-Perez decided not to let Katani enter the United States. It is very likely that Katani was supposed to be the twentieth hijacker.[27] As a result, United Flight 93 had one fewer hijacker than the other three planes.

The Day of the Attack

On September 11, 2001, the nineteen hijackers traveled from different places to avoid suspicion. A computerized screening program selected some of the terrorists for additional security. Those hijackers' luggage was held off the planes until they boarded. But this action had no effect on their plans.

The hijackers on the first two planes, American Fight 11 and United 175, passed through security screening without any problems. They boarded the planes around 7:30 A.M. They sat in first class.

Just before 8:00 A.M., both flights took off from Logan International Airport. At 8:25 A.M., controllers heard the announcement, "We have some planes." Just twenty-one minutes after that, the first plane struck the World Trade Center.

The 9/11 Attack Continues

When Flight 11 struck the North Tower, people in the South Tower felt the impact and saw the fire. But they were told to stay at their desks. In previous emergency situations, many injuries had happened when mobs of people tried to leave at one time. Initially, the Port Authority police thought it was safer for them to remain where they were.

The fire department made a decision to evacuate the entire World Trade Center complex before 9:00 A.M. That was before the second strike. But problems with communication prevented many people from hearing the order.

Stanley Praimnath made his way down to the lobby of the South Tower after the first plane struck the North Tower. A security guard told him that the South Tower was secure and he should go back to his office.[1] At that point, people were not thinking that a second plane would hit. Praimnath returned to his office on the 81st floor. His phone was ringing. It was a colleague calling to see if he was okay. He assured her that he was. Then, looking out his window, he saw United 175 coming straight toward him. The plane was at eye level. He could see the "U" painted on its tail.

"I dropped the phone and I screamed and dove under my desk," he later told investigators. "It was the most ear-shattering sound ever. The plane just crashed into the building. The bottom wing sliced right through the office and it stuck in my office door twenty feet from where I huddled under my desk."[2]

The plane created a cavern from the 77th to 85th floors. A fireball erupted. A blizzard of office papers and flaming debris swirled around the injured buildings. The damage to the South Tower was more severe than to the North Tower. A corner column was severed, and the top of the building leaned to the southeast above the impact. However, unlike in the North Tower, one escape staircase remained open.

Rescued From the Rubble

Brian Clark was one floor above Praimnath when the plane struck. He recalls two noises. The first was the plane hitting the building. The second was the explosion afterwards. He braced himself as the building swayed a long way to the west. For the first ten seconds he was completely terrified.

The lights had gone out. It was dark. Pulling himself together, Clark turned on a flashlight he had put in his pocket after the first plane hit. He looked around. Light fixtures, speakers, and wires dangled from the ceiling. Parts of the concrete floor had buckled. Door frames had fallen out of the walls.

Initially, there were seven people near him who formed a

group. They walked down a level. But then they heard that the floor below was in flames. A debate started as to whether they should go back up to find another way out or continue down. But Clark was not paying attention to the discussion. He had heard a voice.

"Help, help, I'm buried. Is anybody there? Can anybody hear me?"[3] It was Stanley Praimnath.

Praimnath had dug through the rubble and crawled 131 feet until he was stopped by a Sheetrock wall. There he pounded on it. "I'm here. Don't leave me," he yelled.[4]

Most of Clark's group decided to go back up. But Clark grabbed Ron DiFrancesco in order to help Praimnath. He followed Praimnath's voice.

"It was so dark. I just had my flashlight …," Clark recalled. "As I approached him, he was screaming, 'Can you see my hand? Can you see my hand?' And I couldn't until I was literally less than a yard away from him."[5]

Clark moved as much of the rubble away from Praimnath as he could. Then as Praimnath jumped, Clark pulled him out.

"I pulled him over the top and we fell in a heap and hugged. I said, 'I'm Brian,' and he said, 'I'm Stanley.'"[6]

Getting Down

Clark and Praimnath started down the stairs. (DiFrancesco left earlier. He first went up the stairs but later turned around and got out in time.) Water was dripping from broken pipes, making the stairs slippery. Drywall had blown off ceilings and walls. Some of the wallboard lay flat like a slide.

They did not meet anyone until the 68th floor. At that level, the lights were on and the air was not as smoky. Some people were heading back up to help others. Another was waiting with a seriously injured man.

There are amazing stories of people helping others get out of the broken buildings. Mary Jos was on the 78th floor when the

Survivors of the terrorist attacks on the World Trade Center make their way through smoke and debris on September 11, 2001.

plane hit. She was badly burned. A young man named Eric Thompson helped her down seventy-seven flights. She had never met him before. He asked about her family and tried to keep her mind off the pain.

"He talked about everything under the sun other than my injuries. He tried to keep me away from that.... I lost a third of my upper arm. I didn't know how badly I was hurt."[7]

Kelly Reyher was stepping into an elevator on the 78th floor when the attack happened. The impact blasted him inside. The doors all but closed.

"The elevator split at the seams, the floor blew up. You could just sort of look right through the corner of the elevator into the elevator shaft and it was just all fire. And the elevator was filling up with thick, black smoke."[8]

Luckily, there still was a small gap between the doors. Reyher reached through the fire and used his briefcase to pry them open.

Keating Crown and Donna Spera were also on the 78th floor. The impact threw them to the ground. Crown broke his leg and was bleeding from the back of his head. Spera fractured her arm and had other injuries. They were both badly burned.

Reyher, Crown, and Spera helped each other find the exit and get down the stairs. Spera wrapped her arms around Crown and Reyher as they started down. At one point, their passage was blocked by a fallen wall. Crown and Reyher managed to push the wall onto a pipe to create enough space to climb through.

Somewhere along the way, Crown lost Reyher and Spera. He continued down on his own. As he went, word passed in front of him that an injured man was coming. The double line of people squeezed into single file to let Crown through. An unknown man dabbed at his bleeding head with a wet T-shirt. Another woman offered him the last sip of her soda. When Crown reached the sidewalk the paramedics pulled out a metal spring that had lodged in his head. Reyher helped Spera make it the rest of the way down. They came out shortly after Crown.[9]

Not Everyone Could Get Out

Even with a passable stairway, many above the impact were unable to get out. Some people could not find the open exit. Others were trapped by flames, smoke, or fallen debris. Some people chose to go up, hoping for a rooftop rescue that never came.

Stephen Mulderry was with about twelve other people on the 89th floor. He called his brother. "We've tried everything," he said. "We tried to go up. We tried to get down. It's just too hot and it's too much smoke." Then he told his brother that he loved him. It was their last conversation.[10]

Edmund McNally talked to his wife, Liz, three times from inside the South Tower. He was on the 97th floor. He told her how much she meant to him and how much he loved his girls. Then he reminded her about his life insurance policy and told her all the things she would have to do.

"You are a problem solver. You're going to get out of there," Liz told him.

Flowers and messages in the dust decorate the truck of Ladder Company 24 in New York on September 12. The company lost seven firefighters in the attack.

"Liz," he responded. "This was a terrorist attack. I can hear explosions below me."[11]

Other people, who could have made it out, stayed in to help others. Edgar Emery was one of those people. He helped five women get to the stairway and escorted them from the 90th to the 78th floor. They asked him to continue down with them, but he went back up. The women made it out. Emery was later trapped by the smoke and unable to escape.[12]

In the North Tower, Frank De Martini and Pablo Oritz were two more of those heroes. De Martini worked for the Port Authority on the 88th floor of the North Tower. He was the manager of construction and an architect. He was the type of guy who took control of situations. Once he even chased down an armed mugger.[13]

Ortiz was a construction inspector who had always dreamed of working in the World Trade Center. According to his daughter, "When he finally got the job with the Port Authority, he learned the place inside and out."[14]

After the plane hit, De Martini and another Port Authority manager, Mak Hanna, scouted for an exit. They found one. Ortiz and Frank Varriano moved debris out of the way so that people could get to it. Then they helped the people in the area begin their descent.

"If anyone needs medical attention or suffers from asthma, they should go first,"[15] De Martini announced. Judith Reese, who had asthma, began her descent with Jeff Gertler.

Then, armed with a flashlight, crowbar, and walkie-talkie, De Martini and Ortiz went around and freed others trapped in offices and elevators on the floors just below the impact.

Twenty-three people were trapped on the 89th floor. For them, things seemed almost hopeless. The stairway door was jammed shut. The fire was spreading. The corridor was filling up with smoke.

"We were doomed,'" recalled Rick Bryan, one of those trapped. "We had only minutes."[16]

Nathan Goldwasser said he was pounding on the door with some of the others when "almost like a miracle, we heard a voice on the other side yelling, 'Get away from the door!' The next thing, there's a crowbar coming through the wall."[17]

It was De Martini and Ortiz.

They knocked down the door, cleared the blocking debris, and guided the people to the exit. Then De Martini and Ortiz went up to help others. They did not make it out themselves.

Attack on the Pentagon

As people watched the tragedy unfold in New York, another hijacked plane was heading toward Washington, D.C.

American Airlines Flight 77 took off from Washington Dulles Airport at 8:10 A.M. It was headed to Los Angeles, California. The fuel tanks were full. This was true for all the hijacked flights. The hijackers chose long flights so that the fuel tanks would explode with more jet fuel and cause more damage.

At 8:54 A.M., Flight 77 turned southwest. The turn was a deviation from the flight plan. Two minutes later the plane disappeared from radar. A controller in Indianapolis was concerned by what he saw. But he did not know about the other two hijackings. He had not heard the hijackers say, "We have some planes."

The Indianapolis controller reported that Flight 77 was missing and had possibly crashed. They asked the Air Force Search and Rescue at Langley Air Force Base to look for a downed plane. But the aircraft had not crashed. Unnoticed, it had changed course. After learning about the other hijackings, the controller thought his initial assessment might be wrong.

The control center notified the Federal Aviation Administration (FAA) headquarters at 9:24 A.M. that there

Smoke rises from the Pentagon, just outside Washington, D.C., shortly after it was hit by American Airlines Flight 77.

might be a third hijacking. At 9:25 A.M., the control center ordered a ground stop for their region.

Air traffic controllers looked for the missing plane along its original flight path to the west and southwest. But they could not find it. They did not look to the east. That was where the plane was now heading. For thirty-six minutes, Flight 77 traveled toward the U.S. capital undetected.[18]

Barbara Olson called her husband, Ted Olson, the United States solicitor general, from the flight. She told him that hijackers had used knives and box cutters to gain control. They had herded the passengers to the back of the plane. Her husband asked if she could tell where she was. "Over houses," she told him. Someone else on the plane told her they were heading northeast.[19]

When Flight 77 reached Washington, D.C., the airplane made a 330-degree turn. It descended 2,200 feet. Instead of slowing down, the hijackers pushed the throttles to maximum power. Clipping light poles and spraying debris, the Boeing 757 slammed into the Pentagon at about 530 miles per hour.[20] The Pentagon is the headquarters for the U.S. Department of Defense. It is a symbol of the United States' military might.

"I saw this very, very large passenger jet," recalled Terrance Kean, who looked out a nearby window when he heard the plane fly by. "It just plowed right into the side of the Pentagon. The nose penetrated into the portico. And then it sort of disappeared, and there was fire and smoke everywhere."[21]

The building shook when the plane hit. "It wasn't like a rumble, it was just—boom," said Tom Van Leunen of the Navy Public Affairs office. "It immediately put you on your heels, in fact in my case, actually, it kind of knocked me down."[22]

Lieutenant Colonel Art Haubold was also at the Pentagon. "We were sitting there watching the reports on the World Trade Center. All of a sudden, the windows blew in. We could see a fireball out our window."[23]

Patrick Smith heard the blast and then saw a fireball heading toward him. "I dropped to the floor and put my face down. The flame was there and then it was gone. It almost sucked the breath out of you."[24] He waited until the sprinklers came on. Then he made it through the smoky corridors and got out of the building.

The impact demolished floors and shattered glass. Some people became trapped. The resulting fire was so hot that firefighters initially could not get near the blaze. The smell of jet fuel seeped into everything.

Terrible Losses That Could Have Been Worse

Fifty-nine passengers and crew on the plane (excluding the hijackers) and 129 people in the building did not survive. The losses could have been worse. Twenty-four thousand people work at the Pentagon. The plane struck a recently renovated area. Blastproof windows made with KevlarT had been

This photograph, taken early on the morning of September 13, 2001, shows the damage to the Pentagon caused by the plane crash.

installed. Many offices in the area of impact were still empty. These things helped, but the damage was still massive.

The impact area was as wide as a shopping mall and 285 feet deep. Debris was scattered for hundreds of yards. The huge cloud of smoke could be seen for miles.

Truck 105 was the first to get to the Pentagon. Those firefighters were quickly joined by other first responders. Several fire engines were already on the road because of an earlier call that had been canceled. This allowed them to respond faster.

It took five hours of work by hundreds of firefighters to put out the flames surging from the windows. The roof would continue to burn and small fires would flare up even days later. Several times the rescuers were forced to retreat. The first time was because of a partial building collapse. The next three times were because of reports that there were unknown airplanes approaching. While no other airplanes attacked the Pentagon, these reports added to the confusion and panic.

The Collapse

There had been three attacks in less than an hour. Officials were concerned there could be more. At 9:34 A.M., the FAA learned that a fourth plane had been hijacked. It was United Airlines Flight 93, and it was also heading toward Washington, D.C.

At 9:42 A.M., the FAA grounded all flights going in or out of the United States. Never before had officials ordered all air travel in the United States to stop. But there were still planes in the air, and it would take time for them to all land safely.

The State Department, Capitol building, and the White House were all evacuated. The top leaders of the House of Representatives and Senate were taken into federal protection.

Vice President Dick Cheney left his office in the White House just as the plane hit the Pentagon. Secret Service men led him to an underground bunker. From there, he called President George W. Bush.

The president had been reading to children at an elementary school when the first plane struck. His original plan was to return to Washington, D.C. But after the Pentagon was targeted, the Secret Service thought that was too dangerous. Reluctantly, the president agreed to go elsewhere. President Bush boarded Air Force One at around 9:45 A.M. Nine minutes later, Air Force One took to the skies without a fixed destination. They landed at an underground command center in Nebraska.

Police pulled yellow tape across the streets in front of federal buildings. They ordered the tourists out. Around the country, landmarks such as the Washington Monument, Statue of Liberty, and St. Louis Gateway Arch were closed. Other well-known skyscrapers such as the Sears Tower in Chicago were also cleared.

Military jets started flying over Washington, D.C., and New York. Vice President Cheney, with an okay from President Bush, gave the military permission to shoot down commercial aircraft if necessary.[1]

The South Tower Falls

Back in New York, the fires in the World Trade Center were still burning intensely hot. Molten aluminum poured from a corner window on the 80th floor of the South Tower. The plane was melting.[2] Calls from above the impact became more urgent as ceilings and floors collapsed.

When the buildings were designed, engineers thought the structures could withstand the impact of an airplane. But the planes that crashed were much bigger than the ones they had calculated for, and nobody had considered what a fire fed by jet fuel would do to the tower's core. The fire was not hot enough to melt the steel columns. But it was hot enough to soften the metal.

An engineer from the Department of Buildings looked up at the damage from nearby Building 7. He told John Peruggia, an EMS chief, that he was afraid the towers would collapse.[3] Peruggia did not have a radio. He sent a messenger to tell the fire chief.

This was unexpected news. The collapse of a high-rise building was not something the fire department anticipated or trained for. But the warning came too late.

Inside the South Tower, the floors had begun to sag. This pulled the supporting columns inward. The walls lost the ability to bear the load.

At 9:59 A.M., the South Tower seemed to tremble and then it collapsed. The floors slammed against each other as they fell. This forced smoke and debris out windows and other openings.[4] It looked like there were little explosions all the way down. The noise was deafening.

"It started exploding," said Ross Milanytch. He watched the tower fall from the nearby Chase Manhattan Bank. "It was about the 70th floor. And each second another floor exploded out for about eight floors, before the cloud obscured it all."[5]

The collapse took ten seconds. People ran for their lives. Smoke and ash flooded the streets. Dust and debris coated people's clothes and hair. It was difficult to breathe.

"It was a sunny, beautiful morning," recalled Jay Akasi. "And then everything became dark with ash. You couldn't see a foot in front of your face."[6]

Boris Ozersky was trying to calm a panicked woman when the tower began to fall. "I just got blown somewhere, and then it was total darkness.... I was trying to help this woman, but I couldn't find her in the darkness," Ozersky told a reporter.[7]

A man stands amid the dust and debris caused by the towers' collapse, his face covered for protection.

Eventually he did find the woman again. He helped her to a triage center nearby.

The North Tower Falls

Those inside the North Tower felt the South Tower collapse. The building shook when the tower hit the ground. But they did not know what had happened. They could not see that the South Tower was gone unless they were near a window that had been facing it. As a result, the firefighters inside the North Tower had no sense of the urgency. There were orders for the firefighters to leave. But many of these were not heard.

A police helicopter circled above the standing tower. A dispatcher asked the pilot, Tim Hayes, to report on the remaining tower's condition. At 10:07 A.M., Hayes responded. "Advise everybody to evacuate the area in the vicinity of Battery Park City. About fifteen floors down from the top, it looks like it's glowing red.... [The collapse is] inevitable."[8]

The police dispatcher repeated the message several times. But the firefighters did not hear it. The police and firefighter radios operated on different channels.

There were only a few people leaving the building now. Other than rescue workers, those who were still inside were either trapped or had medical conditions that made it difficult to leave.

Jeff Gertler had been helping Judith Reese down the stairs since Frank De Martini found the exit on the 88th floor. Reese had asthma. She could only manage two flights of stairs before having to sit and rest. The smoke and dust made her breathing condition worse.

Rescue workers saw the two of them on the tenth floor. Gertler explained Reese's condition to an officer. The policeman said they would get a chair and carry Reese out. They told Gertler to leave. He offered to walk with them.

The policeman whispered to Gertler, "You don't understand. The building is going to collapse."[9] That sounded crazy. But Gertler left as he had been told to.

At 10:28 A.M., the North Tower collapsed. Gertler made it outside. Reese and those who remained to help her did not. In all, 2,749 people died in the attacks on New York.

Another cloud of smoke and dust rushed through the streets. Afterward, people walked around covered in gray ash like ghosts.

"All that were left of the buildings ... were the steel girders in like a triangular sail shape," said Ross Milanytch. "The dust was about an inch and a half thick on the ground."[10]

America's Mayor

New York Mayor Rudy Giuliani was eating breakfast when he heard about the attack on the North Tower. He rushed to the scene and set up a command center near the site. He was trying to get through to the vice president when the South Tower collapsed. "When I look(ed) around, what I (saw was) something close to a nuclear bomb. I (saw) dark smoke," Giuliani recalled.[11]

The collapse felt like an earthquake. The desks in the command center shook. They needed to evacuate. But the group in the command center had trouble finding a way out. The basement exits were locked. Debris and ash were flying through the air at street level. Finally a couple of building workers led the mayor through an underground passage onto Church Street. From there, Guiliani walked north for two miles. On his way, he talked to reporters and told New Yorkers to remain calm.

Mayor Giuliani was sure and decisive throughout the crisis. He made rapid-fire decisions about rescue operations. He used media outlets to calm and comfort the people of New York. "Tomorrow New York is going to be here," he said in a press conference. "And we're going to rebuild, and we're going to be stronger than we were before.... I want the people of New York to be an example to the rest of the country, and the rest of the world, that terrorism can't stop us."[12]

Later, Giuliani was criticized for a lack of preparation before the attacks and for parts of the responses afterward. But during the crisis, Giuliani portrayed a leadership and compassion that led Oprah Winfrey to call him "America's Mayor."

The Heroes of Flight 93

There were twenty-nine minutes between the collapse of the South Tower and the collapse of the North Tower. During that time, a heroic struggle occurred in the skies above Pennsylvania.

United Airlines Flight 93 took off from the Newark Airport bound for San Francisco at 8:42 A.M. It had been delayed more than twenty-five minutes. The plane took off just four minutes before American Flight 11 hit the North Tower.

For forty-five minutes, the flight seemed routine. Then the hijackers attacked. Air traffic controllers heard the sounds of a struggle through the plane's radio. The captain or first officer shouted, "Hey get out of here—get out of here—get out of here."[13] Then a hijacker made an announcement that a bomb was on board.[14]

Passengers and crew called loved ones from the doomed flight. They learned about the attacks on the other buildings. Tom Burnett talked to his wife.

"There's a group of us who are going to do something," Burnett told her.[15]

Others also called loved ones. Jeremy Glick told his wife that the passengers had taken a vote. They were going to try and take back the plane.[16]

Sandra Bradshaw, a flight attendant, told her husband that some of the passengers were going to rush the hijackers. She was boiling water to throw on them.[17]

At 9:57 A.M. the passengers began storming the cockpit. The cockpit recorder captured the sounds of the assault. There were loud thumps and crashes and the noise of breaking glass and plates.

The hijacker-pilot tried to roll the plane to knock the passengers off balance. But the revolt continued. Finally, one of the hijackers yelled, "Pull it down! Pull it down!"[18]

The plane plowed into an empty field in Shanksville, Pennsylvania at 580 miles per hour.

Emergency workers examine the crater that resulted when United Airlines Flight 93 crashed in a Pennsylvania field. The passengers, hearing of the other attacks, apparently overcame the hijackers, preventing the plane from being used as a weapon.

"I heard this noise like a divebomber.... And the house was shaking," said Paula Pluta. She lived less than a mile from the crash site. Pluta saw the plane plunging at an angle close to 90 degrees. "It looked like a silver bullet," she said.[19]

Trees were knocked down. A fire exploded. The plane left a crater about twenty feet deep.

The aircraft was only about twenty minutes away from Washington, D.C., when it crashed. The hijackers were probably planning to fly the plane into the White House or Capitol.[20] None of the people on board survived. But they had stopped the plane from becoming a missile. They had protected other innocent lives and likely saved a U.S. national symbol.

Aftermath

Shock. Horror. Grief. Anger. Everywhere people were stunned by the size of the attack, the immense devastation, and the huge loss of life. Television stations broadcast nonstop coverage of the attacks. People lined up to donate blood. Doctors and nurses went to clinics and hospitals prepared to treat the injured. But relatively few came. Most of the people who were still inside the towers when they fell died.

Volunteers from around the country came to help with the search and recovery efforts. Donations flooded into the Red Cross and other relief organizations. Those who had loved ones missing held up signs and posted pictures on walls and fences.

They hoped for a miracle. They hoped somehow their loved one survived.

Rescues

A major search and rescue operation began within hours of the collapse. At first, there were a few rescues. Officers John McLoughlin and Will Jimeno were buried in the trade center's underground concourse when the towers fell. They had been working as a team of five. Of the team, they were the only two still alive. "Concrete [was] across my chest, my leg, and a cinder-block wall on my right foot,"[1] Jimeno said later. Neither man could move. They could not even see each other. But they could talk.

Together they reasoned it would be a while before help could get to them. The two men were not sure they could survive for long. Fires burned under the wreckage. Bits of flame crept into the pockets where they were trapped. Luckily the fire did not take hold.

Then as evening came, so did a voice.

Accountant David Karnes had left his office after seeing the attack. He went home, put on his Marine Corps uniform, and went to the site. Karnes and another marine, Sergeant Jason Thomas, started sweeping the area in search of survivors.

"United States Marines. If you can hear us, yell or tap," they called.

Jimeno heard the voices. "Over here![2] PAPD [Port Authority Police Department]. We're here!" he shouted.[3]

The marines followed Jimeno's voice until they were above the place where he was buried.

"Please don't leave us," Jimeno asked.

"I'm not leaving you, buddy." Karnes told him.[4]

The marines stayed, but they had to figure out how to get help. Phone lines in New York City were jammed. Too many people were making calls at one time. Cell phone antennas on top of the World Trade Center had been destroyed. The system could not handle the load.

Karnes managed to get through to his sister in Pittsburgh, Pennsylvania. His sister then called the New York police and fire departments from there. The word got through, and a mass of people came to help.

It took hours to free Jimeno from the rubble. McLoughlin stayed trapped until the next morning. Rescuers worked all night to get him out.

"They thought [my injuries were] so severe they wanted to bring my kids down to see me for the last time," said McLoughlin.[5]

But the fighting spirit that kept both men alive in the rubble kept them alive in the hospital and through several surgeries. Both men survived.

Unfortunately, rescuers did not find many more people alive.

Wreckage

For months, workers slowly removed the mountains of rubble. Machine operators used giant cranes, backhoes, excavators, and shovels to haul away twisted steel and lift heavy pieces of concrete.

There was almost nothing left of the two towers. There were no broken desks, crushed computers, or pieces of carpet. Everything that had once been inside the buildings was an ashy gray powder.

"It's not really right to call it rubble," said Terry Long, who worked as a structural specialist for the Army Corps of Engineers. "It's mostly just steel and dust. If you think how this collapse was pulverizing concrete that can take 3,000 pounds of pressure, well, you don't want to think about it too much."[6]

The area smelled of smoke. Fires still burned. Workers wore gloves, goggles, and dust masks. Some wore respirators. Particles

Sergeant John McLoughlin (seated) and Officer William Jimeno of the
Port Authority Police at a memorial observation six months after 9/11.
The two officers were among the last people rescued from the World
Trade Center after its collapse.

of glass and concrete rubbed against the skin and got into the lungs. Many of the workers would later develop serious breathing problems as a result of the materials they inhaled.

The workers were not only removing the debris. They were carefully searching for evidence and human remains. They kept hoping to find someone alive. But as days went by, that hope grew dim.

In each section, rescuers first searched the ruins for signs of life. Then the machines lifted the large chunks of concrete and steel. Finally officers and others carefully sifted through the dust for body parts. The human remains, at times as small as a finger, were placed in body bags.

"Sometimes you cannot even use shovels," said Steve Welch, a volunteer firefighter. "People are on their knees digging with their hands."[7]

Each layer was carefully examined and removed. "They're taking off inches," said Bill Singerly, a contractor at the site.[8] He had never seen anything like it.

Volunteers passed buckets from one person to another until the bucket reached a dump truck at the end of a line. It was like an old-fashioned bucket brigade to put out a fire, except that the buckets contained dusty debris instead of water.

Search and rescue operations also went on at the Pentagon and in the field where Flight 93 crashed in Pennsylvania. Part of the Pentagon had collapsed. Fires still flared days after. Like the workers in New York, people carefully sorted through the rubble to find remains and evidence.

"My guys are exhausted," said Jerry Crawford, a fire department chief working at the Pentagon crash site. "We're breaking concrete and shoring up walls, ceilings, and columns to make sure they don't collapse on the rescuers as they do their work. It's a slow, methodical process."[9]

In Pennsylvania, a three-mile perimeter was established around the crash site. Volunteers walked shoulder to shoulder looking for anything that did not belong in the woods. They especially wanted to find the cockpit voice recorder and flight data recorder. These "black boxes" would help investigators piece together what had happened inside the plane as it was hijacked and later as it crashed.

In all three sites, medical examiners used DNA to help identify the victims. More than 250 dogs went through rubble, using their sense of smell to help with the recovery. It took six months to remove more than 1.5 million tons of debris from the World Trade Center site. Workers removed another forty-seven thousand tons of rubble from the Pentagon.

A War on Terror

Within a day of the attack, President George W. Bush declared war on terrorism. In a later speech, he said the war would happen on several fronts. It would use "every means of diplomacy, every tool of intelligence, every instrument of law enforcement, [and] every financial influence."[10]

Republicans and Democrats in Congress came together. They issued a joint resolution expressing their outrage at the attack and sympathy for the victims. They promised support and resources for the war on terror.[11] A second resolution authorized the use of force against "nations, organizations, or persons [the president] determines planned, authorized, committed, or aided the terrorist attacks that occurred on September 11, 2001."[12]

For the first time ever, NATO (the North Atlantic Treaty Organization) invoked its mutual defense clause. NATO is a military alliance of twenty-six countries, including the United States. The mutual defense clause says that an attack on one of the countries is an attack against them all.[13]

Countries around the world called to give their sympathy and pledge support. Some countries, such as Great Britain, committed troops to the war on terror. Other countries offered

In the days following 9/11, people put up posters in hopes of finding friends and family members who were missing in the attacks.

information or help with stopping terrorist financing. Still others would assist covert (secret) operations. Pakistan, one of Afghanistan's neighbor, agreed to let the United States use their country and airspace for military operations against their former friends, the Taliban. In so doing, they became a major U.S. partner in the fight against Al Qaeda.

President Bush signed an executive order freezing the money and assets of terrorist organizations and groups that supported them. These organizations would no longer have access to any funds in U.S. banks. President Bush also created the Department of Homeland Security. The new department was responsible for bringing together information and intelligence regarding terrorism. It was also in charge of protecting and strengthening the U.S. food and water systems, transportation, and infrastructure.

A New State of Normal

It took several days for the stock market to reopen in the United States. The New York Stock Exchange (NYSE) is located in lower Manhattan, only a few blocks away from the World Trade Center site. Streets were closed, and it was difficult to get people in and out of the city. Many financial businesses had offices in or near the towers and were devastated by the tragedy. Phone lines and communication systems were damaged. But on Monday, six days after the attack, the U.S. stock exchange reopened.

The resumption of stock trading will "send a very important message to the criminals who so heinously attacked this country," said NYSE Chairman Richard Grasso, "that they lost. The American way of life goes on."[14]

Initially, stocks plummeted. The Dow Jones Industrial Average—a rough measurement of the stock market's overall strength—lost almost 13 percent in the first four days of trading after 9/11.[15] The airlines took the biggest hit. Most of their stocks tumbled 40 to 50 percent.[16]

For months, people were afraid to fly. Congress approved a $15 billion airline bailout. The money funded grants and loans so the carriers could stay in business.

In time, the economy, stock market, and air travel rebounded. Americans returned to their daily activities. But there was a new state of normal. The FAA increased screening and security measures at airports. Emergency personnel trained for disaster situations. The Department of Homeland Security developed an advisory system to communicate the risk of a terrorism strike in the United States. Gone was a sense of security. Terrorism was now a very public and political concern.

An American flag flies at half-staff at the New York Stock Exchange on September 17, 2001, the first day of trading following the attacks.

Muslims in America: Outrage and Fear

"Hate knows no religion. Hate knows no country," said Hamza Yusuf days after 9/11. "Islam was hijacked on that September 11, 2001, on that plane as an innocent victim."[17] Yusuf is a Muslim teacher who had been critical of some U.S. policies. But like many Muslim leaders, he immediately spoke out against the attack.

President Bush also tried to direct the blame away from the Muslim community. He visited a mosque and the Islamic Center of Washington shortly after the attack. He urged respect and tolerance for Arab Americans. He warned against stereotyping Muslims. "The face of terror is not the true faith of Islam," he said. "Islam is peace."[18]

But the messages did not always get through. After 9/11, there was an increase in hate crimes against Middle Eastern Americans. Arab American businesses were robbed and vandalized. There were assaults and even murders of innocent Muslims.

For Muslim families who lost loved ones in the attack, the pain was doubled. Their grief and anger about the attacks was made worse by the fear of prejudice and violence.

Actress Patricia Arquette started a radio campaign to encourage unity and denounce racism. Her father is Muslim, and her mother is Jewish. "Diversity makes America beautiful," she told people.[19]

The Hunt for Bin Laden

Evidence showed that Osama bin Laden was responsible for the 9/11 attacks. President Bush said he wanted bin Laden brought to justice. He recalled the posters from the Old West that said "Wanted: Dead or Alive."[20]

The CIA knew where bin Laden was. He was in Afghanistan, but the Taliban was protecting him. President Bush and Britain's prime minister, Tony Blair, gave the Taliban an ultimatum. They could either "surrender the terrorists or surrender power."[21]

The Taliban chose to fight rather than turn in bin Laden. U.S. air strikes began as night fell on October 7, 2001. Flashes lit up the night sky. Thunderous booms echoed off the surrounding mountains. For about a month, the United States bombed the Taliban defenses and front lines. On December 9, 2001, the last Taliban-held province was conquered.

The United States offered a $25 million reward for bin Laden's capture. The figure increased to $50 million in July 2007. But as of July 2009, bin Laden had not been caught. The surviving members of the Taliban had reorganized and attacked outposts and convoys of Afghan soldiers and police.

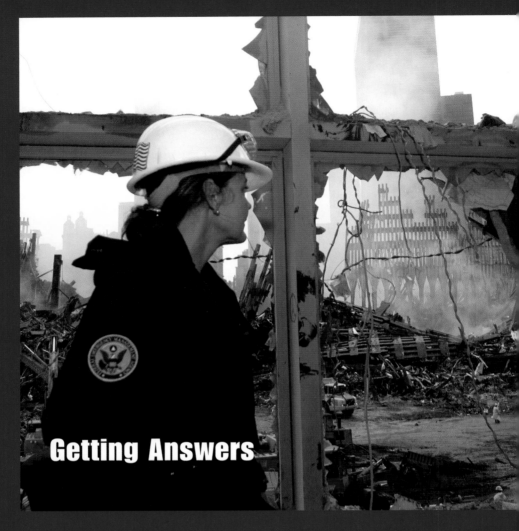

Getting Answers

After the attack, Americans wanted answers. They wanted to know if 9/11 could have been prevented. What had gone wrong? Was there someone to blame? They wanted to find out what the government had done to fight terrorism before the attacks. And they wanted to make the United States safer in the future.

Initially, President Bush opposed the idea of an independent inquiry into the attacks. But the families of the victims lobbied hard for an independent, bipartisan commission. Americans supported the 9/11 families and called their representatives. In November 2002, Congress created the National Commission on Terrorist Attacks upon the United States. It became known as the 9/11 Commission.

There were other questions too. Why had the towers collapsed? Why hadn't more people been rescued? Could high-rise buildings be made safer? The National Institute of Standards and Technology (NIST) began an in-depth investigation to answer these questions.

The 9/11 Commission and the NIST reports would attempt to set the record straight. They would try to give clear accountings of what happened and why. They would also make recommendations for the future.

Some people looked at the available information about the attacks and found errors and discrepancies. Comparisons of timelines between the North American Aerospace Defense Command (NORAD) and the FAA did not make sense. People wondered what had actually happened and if the government was being truthful.

A large amount of airline stock had been traded just days before the attack. Did that mean somebody knew about the attack before it happened? Or had it been a coincidence?

Early on, experts with limited information had speculated about the events and causes. Many of these people were later misquoted or had their quotes taken out of context. This also happened to reporters and eyewitnesses who were sometimes mistaken as they tried to find the right words to describe the events. All these things gave rise to conspiracy theories. A conspiracy theory is a belief a small group of people carried out a secret plot.

Conspiracy Theories

After many big events, conspiracy theories pop up as explanations for gaps in our understanding and differences in information. This was true for such events as the Japanese attack on Pearl Harbor, the assassination of President John F.

Kennedy, and the death of Princess Diana in a car accident. It is also true for the events on 9/11.

Usually a conspiracy theory involves a government cover-up. For the attack on 9/11, some people believe that a government cover-up occurred after the attack to hide failures. Other conspiracy theorists suggest the U.S government had prior knowledge of the attacks and did not stop them. Some theorists even propose that the U.S. government was involved in making the attacks happen.

The evidence for conspiracy theories is often circumstantial (without proof). Even so, these theories persist, and many people believe them. "We tend to associate major events … with major causes," said Patrick Leman, a psychology lecturer who studies conspiracy belief. He explained that the idea of big events caused by an individual or small group unsettles people and makes the world seem unpredictable and scary.[1]

One 9/11 conspiracy theory proposes that the World Trade Center buildings fell because they were wired with explosives. That theory argues that the plane and resulting fire did not do enough damage to cause a full collapse. It states that the collapse looked like a controlled demolition. Another theory suggests that the damage at the Pentagon was actually caused by a missile. A theory regarding Flight 93's crash in Pennsylvania says the plane was shot down by the U.S. military. Sometimes conspiracy theories develop to unfairly blame a group of people. After 9/11, an anti-Semitic (or anti-Jewish) claim surfaced that four thousand Jews were warned of the attack and had not gone to work. This was easy to prove false, but there are still people who believe it.

Several sources have refuted the claims and offered explanations for the questions conspiracy theorists raise. The 9/11 Commission examined thousands of documents and found no evidence for these theories. This is also true of the NIST report in which experts explained how and why the towers collapsed.[2]

In 2005, the magazine *Popular Mechanics* examined the most common 9/11 conspiracy theories. They consulted with more than three hundred experts for their story. In the end, the researchers discredited each theory with what they called "hard evidence and a healthy dose of common sense."[3]

Designing the World's Tallest Buildings

When the Twin Towers were built in the early 1970s, they were the world's tallest buildings. Engineers used innovative techniques in order to make them that tall. Previous skyscrapers had relied on interior columns to support most of the weight. However, the Twin Towers used closely spaced columns of high-quality steel on the outside of the buildings to hold the load. Interior columns were only needed around the central core that contained the pipes, elevators, and stairwells. This design change increased the amount of rentable space in the buildings.

The Twin Towers also used a new approach for moving people. The elevators worked like a vertical subway. Express elevators zipped up to sky lobbies on the 44th and 78th floors. There people could take shorter, local elevators to the floor they wanted. This design meant that fewer elevators were needed, and people could get to their floors faster. Each tower had ninety-nine elevators. People took 450,000 combined rides in the World Trade Center elevators each day.[4]

Changes in the 1968 building codes allowed designers to include fewer stairways and reduce the amount of protection around them. Each tower had only three sets of stairs. The stairways and elevators were close together in the core of the building. The designers never planned for a full evacuation. They assumed that any need for an evacuation could be limited to a smaller number of floors.

This was a problem on September 11. When the first plane struck the North Tower, it severed the stairwells and damaged the elevators. People above the impact had no way down.

New York City firefighters and rescue workers from the Federal Emergency Management Agency search through the rubble for victims. Changes in building codes allowed the towers to have fewer stairways than other high-rise structures. This contributed to evacuation problems on September 11.

The steel exterior columns, elevators, stairwells, and evacuation were just some of the things NIST investigated after the collapse. Their task was to figure out why and how the buildings fell. They were also supposed to look at the loss of life and difficulties with the evacuation and emergency response. Finally, they were to recommend ways to make buildings safer.

The NIST Investigation

Usually, when NIST investigates the damage to a building, there is a building left to examine. The Twin Towers were mainly reduced to dust. NIST would have to find other ways to research what happened. S. Shyam Sunder was NIST's lead investigator for the World Trade Center disaster. "It's very unusual that evidence is so completely scattered," he told a *NOVA* documentary. "That made our investigation a lot more complicated."[5]

Researchers collected documents on the design, construction, operation, and maintenance of the towers. They sent out a request for photos and video footage of the events. Engineers reviewed more than seven thousand pictures and more than one hundred fifty hours of film. They interviewed more than a thousand witnesses and collected 236 pieces of steel from the World Trade Center site for testing.

Then the engineers used state-of-the-art computer programs to model what had happened to the buildings. "We had to model the complete aircraft impact. We had to model the evolution of the fires over the next hour or hour and a half. We had to model how the steel weakened as a result of the higher temperatures. And lastly we had to model the progression of local failures in the structure which then led to the overall initiation of collapse," explained Sunder.[6]

Why the Towers Fell

NIST determined that the fall of the Twin Towers was due to a combination of three factors: the damage caused by the impact, the dislodging of fireproofing that protected the steel, and the uncontrollable multifloor fire.

The planes plowed into the exterior columns and broke apart. Debris scattered throughout four to six floors. Some pieces of the airplanes, such as the landing gear from Flight 11 and an engine component from Flight 175, traveled all the way through the buildings and were found on the other side.[7]

The crashes also took out several of the interior columns around the buildings' core. In the North Tower, six of the columns were severed, and three were severely damaged. In the South Tower, the plane severed ten columns and severely damaged one.

As the planes cut through the buildings, they dislodged the fireproofing around the floor trusses. The puffy fireproofing had been sprayed on the steel to protect it from high-temperature fires. The energy from the impact blew it off.

The jet fuel in the planes ignited, and a huge fire followed. The jet fuel burned off within about ten minutes, but the fire continued to burn, fueled by desks, workstations, carpets, and other flammable materials. Air flowing through the broken windows supplied oxygen for the fire. The impact also damaged the water pipes, causing the sprinkler system to fail.

The buildings probably would not have fallen if the fire-proofing had not been dislodged or if the fire could have been controlled. Without the fireproofing, the steel weakened as a result of the intense heat. This caused the floors to sag and the columns to bow inward. Eventually the columns snapped, and the floors above started moving downward. The structure below could not withstand the energy released. This caused the buildings to collapse.

Some people wondered why the South Tower collapsed sooner than the North Tower. One reason was because of where the plane hit the building. The second plane took out core columns in the southeast corner. Removing the corner columns made the South Tower more unstable.

"It's like looking at a three- or four-legged stool and essentially taking out one leg," said Sunder.[8] Another reason was that a fire burned in one place on the east face of the second building for a long time. That also shortened the amount of time before the building fell.

After completing their review, NIST made recommendations

for high-rise safety. The recommendations included ideas for strengthening the structural design, improving evacuations, and helping emergency response. They suggested expanding stair-wells to accommodate more people, increasing fire protection, and improving internal communication and access for first responders.

More Than the Towers

The World Trade Center was more than the two towers. It was a complex of seven different buildings. All seven buildings were destroyed in the attack. The Twin Towers were the best known. Climbing more than a quarter of a mile high, they had been focal points in the New York skyline.

The Marriott World Trade Center hotel was a twenty-two-story building located between the towers. It connected the two towers through a concourse area and was used as a staging area for emergency responders during the crisis. The hotel was cut in half when the South Tower collapsed and completely crushed by the fall of the North Tower. It is estimated that fifty people died in the hotel. At least forty-one of them were firefighters.[9]

Building 7 stood for close to seven hours after the towers collapsed. During that time, a fire raged inside. At 5:20 P.M., the forty-seven-story building also gave way. Fortunately, the build-ing had been evacuated, and no one died when it fell.

Early reports by FEMA (Federal Emergency Management Agency) said that the damage to Building 7 was relatively light. But photographic evidence shows that the initial FEMA report was mistaken. There had been significant damage to the building's south face. According to S. Shyam Sunder, on "approximately 10 stories [of Building 7] about 25 percent of the depth of the building was scooped out."[10]

The other three World Trade Center buildings had severe structural damage as a result of the attack. They were later torn down.

The 9/11 Commission

"We were set up to fail," thought Thomas Kean as he prepared to meet Lee Hamilton for the first time.[11] President Bush had appointed Thomas Kean as chairman of the 9/11 Commission. Lee Hamilton was chosen for vice chairman by the Democrats. Neither man had been their party's first choice. Hamilton looked at the commission's mandate and thought the same thing as Kean. The odds of making it work were stacked against them.

The commission's task was huge. It was supposed to examine the intelligence agencies, law enforcement, diplomacy, immigration, border control, how the terrorists moved money, commercial aviation, congressional oversight, resources spent on counterterrorism, and anything else they found relevant to the attacks on 9/11. They were supposed to give a clear account of what happened that day and in the weeks and months beforehand. Then they would make recommendations based on what they learned to help stop a future attack.

The commission had a very short window of time to complete its work and not enough money. Perhaps the biggest obstacle was politics. Republicans and Democrats were deeply divided in Congress. For the commission to succeed, the five Republican and five Democratic commissioners would need to give up party politics, work together, and eventually agree.

Fortunately, Kean and Hamilton immediately liked each other. Together they decided that they would be unyielding in discovering the facts. They would make the proceedings as open as possible and demand to see everything they asked for. They chose not to assign individual blame. Instead they would focus on institutional problems. This bothered some of the 9/11 family members. But assigning blame would have set the Republicans and Democrats against each other. The 9/11 Commission would be the fact finder. Afterward, others could assign blame based on their facts.

Former New Jersey governor Thomas Kean (left) and former Indiana congressman Lee Hamilton headed up the 9/11 commission. Both men were concerned about the commission's ability to perform the huge task ahead.

Testimony

The commission opened with emotional testimony. Both survivors of the attack and family members of those who died told the commission about their suffering and loss.

Harry Waizer was one of the survivors who spoke. His face was badly scarred from the burns he had suffered in a World

Trade Center elevator. The firm he worked for, Cantor Fitzgerald, lost 658 employees in the attack.

Waizer described being in the elevator as it plummeted. Orange sparks were streaming through the gaps in the doors. He spoke about the fireball that had hit him in the face, burning his skin and searing his windpipe and lungs. He told the commissioners about his recovery. He had spent five months in the hospital, six or seven weeks in an induced coma. He had gone through multiple surgeries and painful therapy. He was at the hearing to speak for those who could no longer and to challenge the 9/11 Commission to succeed. He said:

> If the findings of this commission can prevent even one future 9/11, if they can forestall even one plan of Osama bin Laden, prevent even one more act of madness and horror, I and the rest of this nation will owe the commission our gratitude, and I will be proud of the small part I was allowed to play today.[12]

Waizer did not express anger. He stated that the perpetrators were "not worthy of my rage."[13] They were madmen who must be stopped. But Steve Push testified about his unyielding fury. His wife was killed aboard Flight 77. He believed the attack was preventable. He told the commission to "ask the tough questions and offer tough solutions."[14]

Subpoenas

In the following weeks, the commission staff began the huge task of requesting and reviewing materials. At first, the commission simply asked for the documents it needed to see. When they met roadblocks, the 9/11 families stepped in and applied political pressure. Americans were outraged when it seemed that people or agencies were not cooperating with the review. The commission usually got what it wanted. But it also had another tool it could use. Congress had given the commission the right to subpoena information. A subpoena is a court order for evidence. The threat of the subpoena made the administration more likely to heed their document requests. When all else failed, the commission issued subpoenas to gain the necessary information.

The first subpoena went to the FAA. More than once the FAA had supplied incomplete materials to the commission staff. The staff wanted the records so they could tell the public how events occurred. They also needed to clear up the timeline discrepancies between the FAA and military defense command. The second subpoena went to the Defense Department. Specifically, the commission wanted the information from NORAD.

The subpoenas forced the agencies to hand over the information in a complete and timely fashion. It would have been embarrassing to appear not to cooperate.

The commission's final report clarified the timelines. The tapes and documents showed that the military had been confused about how many planes were hijacked and about which plane was which. Six minutes was the longest amount of time that NORAD had between learning about a hijacking and the plane's impact. That was for the first plane. Military jets had been launched, but the pilots had not known where to go. The shoot-down order had not been fully communicated. The commission concluded that NORAD had not had enough time to react to the threats or shoot down the planes.

This information refuted a conspiracy theory that the U.S. military could have acted but had been ordered not to. It also showed weaknesses in the U.S. defense systems that would have to be addressed. Before 9/11, the defense systems pointed outward. The expectation was that an attack would come from outside the country. The United States was not prepared to handle a threat from within.

The commission also investigated the airline stock trading

prior to 9/11. They found no evidence of wrongdoing or that anyone involved had prior knowledge of the attack.

Access to Presidents

Never before had a commission asked to see the range or number of classified presidential documents that the commission wanted to review. They asked to see internal National Security Council documents, presidential directives, covert action reports, internal memos, minutes of meetings, and presidential daily briefings (PDBs). There were security risks if the information got out. But Kean and Hamilton knew they needed to see everything they requested. Seeing anything less would add fuel for conspiracies.

The commission could subpoena these documents. But there was a question whether the information would be subject to executive privilege. Executive privilege is the idea that a president has the right to keep certain documents confidential to protect national security. It also allows the president to get candid advice without his staff worrying that this advice will later be shown to Congress. A court case to determine whether or not the documents would be released would have taken longer than the commission's term.

However, President Bush did not want to look like he had anything to hide. Complex negotiations took place about how many people could see the material and under what security precautions. Certain commissioners were given clearance, and in the end the 9/11 Commission saw everything it asked to see.

The commission also interviewed President Bush, Vice President Cheney, and former President Bill Clinton. Many other officials testified too. These included Secretaries of State Madeleine Albright and Colin Powell, Attorneys General Janet Reno and John Ashcroft, Secretaries of Defense William Cohen and Donald Rumsfeld, Security Advisors Samuel "Sandy" Berger and Condoleezza Rice, Counterterrorism Advisor

President George Bush and First Lady Laura Bush lay a wreath in memory of those who died on United Airlines Flight 93 in Pennsylvania. Bush initially opposed the idea of a 9/11 Commission, but later provided the information members requested.

Richard Clarke, CIA Director George Tenet, FBI Director Robert Mueller, and many more.

In the end, the 9/11 Commission set down a record of events that all the commissioners signed and agreed on. It was a demonstration of democracy at its finest. The American people had asked for the commission. Congress had responded and created a mandate. The president had signed the bill. Five Republicans and five Democrats had come together as independent citizens. They had asked to see volumes of information and saw everything they requested. They had interviewed government officials in open and public arenas. Then all ten commissioners had come to a consensus about what had happened and what could make the United States safer.

As Kean and Hamilton noted:

> Our system is not always efficient, effective, or wise, and it can stand improvement, but it is a system worth defending abroad, and advancing here at home. Where else could ten independent citizens probe the inner workings of a government, question everybody up to a sitting president of the United States, and engage in a national dialogue on the key question of the day?[15]

The Commission's Findings

The commission members knew they were looking at the events on 9/11 with hindsight. What was clear after the attack was not clear beforehand. They acknowledged the dedication of the people who fight terrorism in such agencies as the CIA and FBI. They noted that the FAA had been able to clear U.S. airspace and bring all the nonhijacked flights to the ground safely in a very short period of time. On 9/11, people were improvising a defense. No one had trained for an event like this.

First responders had bravely entered the burning towers of the World Trade Center. Around 17,400 people were in the towers that morning. Ninety-nine percent of those who worked below the impact zone had gotten out safely.[16]

The report called the inability to stop the attacks a failure of imagination.[17] Leaders had not understood how great a threat Al Qaeda posed. They did not realize how innovative its operatives were. Not enough importance or resources were given to counterterrorism.

Specific problems occurred in many areas, including U.S. policy, intelligence, diplomacy, aviation security, border control, and communication. There is no way of knowing what combination of actions would have stopped the 9/11 attacks. The terrorists were both flexible and resourceful. However, the 9/11

Commission did find specific points at which opportunities to discover and disrupt the plot were missed.

Missed Opportunities

The CIA had both plans and opportunities to capture or kill bin Laden in the late 1990s. The last, best opportunity before the attack was in May 1999. The CIA had solid intelligence that bin Laden was in Kandahar, a city in southern Afghanistan. The information was detailed. The cruise missiles were ready. But the decision was made not to strike. Officials worried about the collateral (additional) damage the attack might cause to innocent civilians. They were also concerned about diplomatic problems that might result, and some had doubts about the quality of the intelligence.

U.S. Customs officer Jose Melendez-Perez stopped terrorist Mohamed al Katani from entering the United States at the

Jose Melendez-Perez, a customs and border inspector, testified in front of the 9/11 Commission. He is credited with preventing one of the intended hijackers from entering the United States.

border. The commission found other ways that terrorists could have been prevented from entering the country. Many of the terrorists carried altered or suspicious passports. They made false statements on their applications and to border officials. Some of the terrorists were known Al Qaeda operatives who could have been put on a watch list. Before 9/11, protecting the borders was not a major part of counterterrorism efforts. It was an area that needed improvement.

Some opportunities were missed because intelligence agencies had not shared information. The CIA had evidence that Nawaf al Hazmi and Khalid al Mihdhar, hijackers aboard Flight 77, were tied to Al Qaeda and the attack on the U.S.S. *Cole*. They also knew the two men had U.S. visas. But the CIA's focus was outside the United States. The FBI was responsible for investigations inside the country. Rules about sharing information were complicated, and there was a lot of confusion about them. Agents sometimes called these rules the "wall." The rules had been designed to protect evidence for criminal cases and prevent intelligence investigations from being abused. But they proved disastrous on 9/11. The FBI did not start looking for the hijackers until it was too late.

The commission hoped that by looking at mistakes they could find ways to make the United States safer. The 9/11 report included a list of recommendations for "what to do" and "how to do it."

"We propose a strategy with three dimensions," the 9/11 Commission wrote in the executive summary. "(1) Attack terrorists and their organizations, (2) prevent the continued growth of Islamist terrorism, and (3) protect against and prepare for terrorist attacks."[18]

The likelihood of being killed in a terrorist attack is very small. People are more likely to die from falling off a ladder (a chance of one in 7,990)[1] than in a terrorist attack (one in 88,000).[2] The odds of dying from a lightning strike (one in approximately 80,000)[3] are greater than dying from terrorism. Even in 2001, car accidents killed fifteen times more Americans than the attack on 9/11.[4]

One goal of terrorism is to instill fear. America's sense of safety was severely shaken after 9/11. Experts often say that terrorists create a theater for their attacks. Terrorists want an audience. The more viewers they have, the more terror they create.

The heightened fear is also a result of the unpredictability of terrorism. "We like things to be in our control or in our imagined control," said Stevan Hobfoll, a psychologist specializing in the stress of terrorism. "Of course, terrorism is well outside of our control."[5]

Because of this, the fear of terrorism is often out of proportion to the actual threat. That does not mean people should be unconcerned. But people need to keep the threat of terrorism in perspective.

"I don't think the terrorists are as plentiful or as powerful as some people would suggest," said John Brennan, a CIA veteran and former head of the National Counterterrorism Center. "They are very dangerous. And it only takes one cell to do tremendous damage, or cause significant loss of life. But I think that sometimes the terrorist threat is overstated, giving one the impression that terrorists are everywhere to be found. That's not the case."[6]

Reducing the Risk

After 9/11, stopping terrorism became a priority. Around the world, people are working to reduce the risk of terrorist attacks.

Through diplomacy, the United States works with allies to create international laws that will stop terrorists from recruiting or raising money. Governments also work together to put political and financial pressure on countries that support terrorism or ignore terrorist organizations operating within their borders.

The military is sometimes used to topple regimes that back terror organizations such as the Taliban in Afghanistan. The military may also go after terrorists directly, such as hunting for Osama bin Laden.

Getting good intelligence is key to counterterrorism efforts, says Dan Byman, director of the Center for Peace and Security Studies at Georgetown University. "Arresting or killing terrorists is often the easy part. The hard part is finding them."[7]

The CIA and other intelligence agencies employ human spies, intercept phone calls, locate terrorist camps with satellites, and use other means to find and track terrorists. They monitor activities to better understand how the organizations work and to stop terror plots before they happen.

Boosting a nation's defenses is another part of counterterrorism. Defenses include things such as screening airline passengers, strengthening cockpit doors, searching imported goods, and monitoring borders. "Defenses don't stop terrorists directly, but they do make it harder for them to win," said Byman. "It's like football. You don't win the game with defense alone, but you need defense to stop the other side from winning."[8]

Since 9/11, the amount of money available to fight terrorism has greatly increased. Security has improved at borders, airports, seaports, and other places terrorists might want to attack. Countries are working together and sharing information to defeat terrorism. Threats are monitored. About 150 countries have frozen terrorist-related financial assets.[9]

"No instrument solves all of the problems," said Byman. "They must all be used, and constantly modified."[10]

Is the United States Safer?

In December 2004, Congress passed the Intelligence Reform and Terrorism Prevention Act. The bill reorganized the nation's security to address the new dangers of terrorism. But the passage of the law was only a first step.

In November 2005, the 9/11 Commission issued a report card on the progress the United States had made in the fight against terrorism. They had seen positive steps toward carrying out the commission's recommendations, but they still saw areas that needed improvement. There were forty-one letter grades in the evaluation. The highest grade was an A- for the efforts to

The War in Iraq

In October 2002, President Bush used the War on Terror as reason to invade Iraq. He believed that the president of Iraq, Saddam Hussein, might be developing nuclear weapons that could be used in terrorist attack.

Saddam Hussein was a ruthless dictator. He had used chemical weapons during the Iraq-Iran War and later used them to kill Iraqi Kurds who had opposed his rule. However, weapons inspectors had not found specific evidence that Iraq had nuclear weapons.

In March 2003, U.S. forces, with the support of several allies, began military operations in Iraq. After close to three months of air strikes, President Bush declared that major combat operations had ended. However, the problems were just beginning. Small groups of rebels known as insurgents began attacking U.S. and Iraqi security forces with homemade bombs known as IEDs (improvised explosive devices). Later these attacks began targeting Iraqi civilians.

As violence increased, U.S. citizens questioned the decision to go to war. No nuclear weapons were found within the country. The 9/11 Commission found no connection between Saddam Hussein and Al Qaeda or the 9/11 attacks. In 2006, a U.S. intelligence report found that the Iraq War had made the terrorist threat to the United States worse.[11]

stop terrorist financing. There were twelve Bs, nine Cs, ten Ds, and five Fs. Two areas were incomplete.[12]

Some of the most important 9/11 Commission recommendations will not be made with laws. These recommendations are for how the United States relates with Islamic countries. The commission suggested that the United States engage in more diplomacy, dialogue, and education.

Five years after 9/11, a U.S. government report declared, "Though America and its allies are safer ... we are not yet safe."[13]

"Terrorism has been around for millennia and is not likely to go away," says Byman. "But it can be brought down to a tolerable level.... If people panic and overreact to terrorism, it often plays into the hands of radicals. Similarly, a failure to respond at all can embolden terrorists. Democratic societies must walk a fine line but we can, in the end, emerge triumphant."[14]

Finding Ways to Remember

Thousands of people died in the attacks on 9/11. Afterward, there were thousands of funerals. Flags across the country were lowered to half-staff. People gathered together for candlelight vigils.

St. Paul's Chapel, an Episcopal church, stands directly across from the World Trade Center site. The church was built in 1766. President George Washington worshiped there on his inauguration day in 1789. Somehow the church survived the attack. Not even a window was broken. The fence that surrounds it became an instant memorial to the victims of 9/11. People left photos, flowers, teddy bears, flags, and other personal remembrances there.

During the recovery, the chapel also became a place of rest and refuge for people working at the World Trade Center site. Volunteers provided everything from cots to rest on and food to eat to massages and counseling. Eventually the fence was cleared of the personal items. But the church continues to be a place where people visit to remember those who died in the attacks. Inside the church are several 9/11 exhibits, including memorial banners and extensive audiovisual history.

Six months after the attack, a Tribute in Light was erected where the towers once stood. Eighty-eight floodlights created two beams that could be seen on a clear night more than twenty-five miles away. It was as if the towers, which once stood 110 stories tall, now stretched all the way to heaven. The tribute was displayed from dusk until 11:00 P.M. for thirty-two days and has been recreated on the anniversaries of the attack in 2003–2008.

St. Paul's Chapel became a place of refuge for workers after the attacks. Today it houses exhibits and memorials.

Remembering Flight 93

On September 10, 2002, both houses of Congress passed a bill that created a national memorial to the heroes of Flight 93. The memorial is being built in the field where the plane crashed. The crash site is considered sacred ground. The memorial also includes a park of about twelve hundred acres and a wetlands habitat filled with life that will symbolize healing.

The winning design includes a "tower of voices" at the entrance. A tall metallic arc will house forty wind chimes—one for each of the victims. Wind in the area is almost a constant, so the chimes will ring as a reminder of the voices lost. A grove of red maple trees will surround the memorial. A clearing will mark the flight's path. In the clearing, a white stone slab will provide an entryway to the sacred ground for visitors. The names of the forty victims will be inscribed in white marble on the western wall.

Remembering Flight 77 and the Victims at the Pentagon

Inside the reconstructed wing of the Pentagon is a dimly lit memorial and chapel. Large black panels list the names of those who died there on 9/11. An adjacent wall has the Purple Heart medal, which was awarded to military members killed in the attack. Another panel displays the Defense of Freedom medal given to the civilians who died in the Pentagon.

Outside the Defense headquarters there is a larger memorial. In it, 184 benches will represent the 184 innocent lives that were lost as Flight 77 hit the Pentagon. Each metal bench is cantilevered, like a diving board, above a small pool of water and is inscribed with the name of a victim. Fifty-nine benches face one direction, representing the passengers on Flight 77. One hundred twenty-five face the other direction, for those who died inside the Pentagon. Red maples have been planted throughout the close to two-acre memorial. Soon they will grow and provide shade and privacy for those who visit.

Remembering Flights 11 and 175 and the Victims in the World Trade Center

The first large-scale permanent memorial near the World Trade Center was a fifty-six-foot-long bronze relief dedicated to the 343 firefighters who died on 9/11. In the center are the burning towers. On either side firefighters are shown responding to the tragedy. The names on it can be touched and traced by visitors and loved ones. The inscription reads: "Dedicated to those who fell and to those who carry on. May we never forget."[15]

By far, the greatest loss of life was at the World Trade Center. There, the memorial has been the hardest to design and build.

Six months after 9/11, the Tribute in Light was erected where the towers stood. Here a little boy who lost his mother at the World Trade Center points to the beams of light.

The grief and loss are immense. But area residents want their neighborhood to remain a living place and not resemble a cemetery. The property is very valuable. The cost of the memorial has been an issue. And even the families have not agreed on what should be memorialized.

Out of more than five thousand entries, a design was chosen using the footprints of the towers to reflect their absence. The two spaces where the towers stood will remain empty except for a cascading waterfall descending into a pool of water and the names of the victims. Below the street, at pool level, will be a museum. Two galleries will let people view the original perimeter columns and a section of the foundation. There will also be artifacts that survived the fire and towers' fall, such as the last column recovered from the buildings.

A long flight of stairs that was used by many as an escape route also survived the collapse. It will be incorporated into the museum's entrance. Visitors will walk alongside the "survivor's stairs" as they descend to the museum. "The stairs are a potent reminder of the path to salvation and survival that many people had," said Avi Schick, chief of downtown redevelopment.[16] Walking beside them, visitors will be more aware of what it must have been like to evacuate the buildings.

Next to the memorial, a new building will reach to the sky. The Freedom Tower will be the tallest of five skyscrapers built to replace the World Trade Center complex. The Freedom Tower will rise to 1,776 feet. The spire is designed to resemble the Statue of Liberty's torch and will be lit at night. At its base, a block of marble reads: "To honor and remember those who lost their lives on September 11, 2001 and as a tribute to the enduring spirit of freedom, July Fourth 2004."[17]

The building's design is also a tribute to those who died. Many safety features have been incorporated. These include a separate staircase for emergency responders; thicker, stronger walls around the air shafts, water pipes, stairs, and elevators; better fireproofing; extra structural support to prevent collapse; and the use of special glass for the lobby that can survive blasts.

Remembering as a Nation

The attacks of 9/11 affected the United States as a nation. Family members of those who died, the passengers aboard the planes, and those who worked in the buildings came from all over the United States and from more than ninety different countries. Smaller memorials have been built in many different states. Some of the memorials include pieces of twisted steel from the towers. Some are statues. Others are nameplates dedicating fountains, trees, flagpoles, and parks to the memory of those who perished. Streets were named after victims, and songs were written and performed at memorial concerts.

Rick Cahill lost his son in the North Tower when it collapsed. Less than a year later, he spoke at a memorial that was being dedicated to his son and two others who had died on 9/11. He asked people to remember more than just the tragedy. He asked people to remember "how we felt when we became one as a community, in caring thoughtfulness for one another."[18]

Timeline

September 11, 2001

> **8:46 A.M.**—American Airlines Flight 11 hits the North Tower
>
> **9:03 A.M.**—United Flight 175 hits the South Tower
>
> **9:25 A.M.**—FAA grounds all flights going in or out of the United States
>
> **9:37 A.M.**—American Airlines Flight 77 hits the Pentagon
>
> **9:59 A.M.**—South Tower collapses
>
> **10:03 A.M.**—United Airlines Flight 93 crashes in a field in Shanksville, Pennsylvania
>
> **10:28 A.M.**—North Tower collapses
>
> **5:20 P.M.**—WTC Building 7 collapses

September 12, 2001—President George W. Bush declares the terrorist attack an act of war

September 17, 2001—U.S. stock market reopens for the first time after the attack

October 7, 2001—Air strikes begin against the Taliban in Afghanistan

March 11, 2002—The Tribute in Light is first created on the WTC site

August 15, 2002—Workers move into the rebuilt offices at the Pentagon

November 15, 2002—Congress creates the 9/11 Commission

July 22, 2004—9/11 Commission releases its report

September 2005—NIST releases its *Final Report on the Collapse of the World Trade Center Towers*

June 10, 2006—FDNY Memorial Wall is dedicated

September 11, 2008—Memorial at the Pentagon is completed

September 11, 2011—Reflecting Absence, New York memorial, projected opening

September 11, 2011—Memorial to Flight 93 in Somerset County, Pennsylvania, projected opening

Chapter Notes

Chapter 1 The Sky Turns Dark

1. Tom Brokaw, "The skies over America: The air traffic controllers on 9/11 saw the nightmare coming," *MSNBC*, September 9, 2006, <http://www.msnbc.msn.com/id/14754701/> (February 3, 2009).

2. Ibid.

3. National Commission on Terrorist Attacks Upon the United States, *The 9/11 Commission Report: Final Report of the National Commission on Terrorist Attacks Upon the United States*, authorized edition (New York: W. W. Norton & Company, 2004), p. 19.

4. Ibid.

5. Brokaw.

6. Ibid.

7. Ibid.

8. National Commission on Terrorist Attacks Upon the United States, p. 20.

9. Brokaw.

10. "Betty Ong's Call from 9/11 Flight 11," The Memory Hole, March 2, 2004, <http://www.thememoryhole.org/911/911-ong-tape.htm> (February 3, 2009).

11. National Commission on Terrorist Attacks Upon the United States, *Staff Report*, August 26, 2004, <http://www.archives.gov/legislative/research/9-11/staff-report-sept2005.pdf> (February 3, 2009).

12. Ibid.

13. National Institute of Standards and Technology, *Final Report on the Collapse of the World Trade Center Towers*, September 2005, <http://wtc.nist.gov/NCSTAR1/PDF/NCSTAR%201.pdf> (April 5, 2009).

14. Jim Dwyer and Kevin Flynn, *102 Minutes: The Untold Story of the Fight to Survive Inside the Twin Towers* (New York: Times Books, 2006), p. 18.

15. *New York Times*, "Accounts From the North Tower," May 26, 2002, <http://www.nytimes.com/2002/05/26/nyregion/26NTOWER.html?ex=1181793600&en=2e2fe12044ca1fd0&ei=5070> (February 3, 2009).

16. Dwyer and Flynn, p. 39.

17. Ibid.

18. *New York Times*, "Accounts From the North Tower."

19. Ibid.

20. Ibid.

21. Stephen Collinson, "'it is very hot, I am going to die aren't i,'" *National Post*, Don Mills, Ontario, April 11, 2006, p. A3.

22. Al Baker and James Glanz, "For 911 Operators, Sept. 11 Went Beyond All Training," *New York Times*, April 1, 2006, p. A1, <http://www.nytimes.com/2006/04/01/nyregion/01operator.html?pagewanted=2&ei=5070&en=a533efc81db58865&ex=1181793600> (February 3, 2009).

23. Dwyer and Flynn, p. 47.

24. Ibid., p. 172.

25. CBS News, *What We Saw—The Events of September 11, 2001, in Words, Pictures, and Video* (New York: Simon & Schuster, 2002), p. 16.

26. Ibid., p. 18.

27. "Campaign Against Terror—Interview: Condoleezza Rice," *Frontline*, July 12, 2002, <http://www.pbs.org/wgbh/pages/frontline/shows/campaign/interviews/rice.html> (February 3, 2009).

Chapter 2 Osama Bin Laden and the Threat of Al-Qaeda

1. "Bin Laden's Fatwa," *Online News Hour*, n.d., <http://www.pbs.org/newshour/terrorism/international/fatwa_1996.html> (February 3, 2009).

2. Lynn Ludlow, "Osama speaks: Inside the mind of a terrorist," *San Francisco Chronicle*, October 7, 2001, p. D1, <http://www.sfgate.com/cgi-bin/article.cgi?file=/chronicle/archive/2001/10/07/IN176521.DTL> (February 3, 2009).

3. Michael Scheuer, *Through Our Enemies' Eyes: Osama bin Laden, Radical Islam, and the Future of America*, revised edition (Dulles, Va.: Potomac Books Inc., 2006), p. 89.

4. David Von Drehle, "A Lesson in Hate," *Smithsonian.com*, February 2006, <http://www.smithsonianmag.com/history-archaeology/presence-feb06.html> (February 3, 2009).

5. National Commission on Terrorist Attacks Upon the United States, *The 9/11 Commission Report: Final Report of the National Commission on Terrorist Attacks Upon the United States*, authorized edition (New York: W. W. Norton & Company, 2004), p. 51.

6. Ibid., p. 54.

7. U.S. Department of State, *Did the U.S. "Create" Osama bin Laden?* <http://beijing.usembassy-china.org.cn/creating_laden.html> (April 5, 2009).

8. Peter L. Bergen, *Holy War, Inc.: Inside the Secret World of Osama bin Laden* (New York: Free Press, 2001), p. 61.

9. Scheuer, pp. 155–156.

10. "Eliminating Terrorist Sanctuaries: The Role of Security Assistance" (Hearing Before the Subcommittee on International Terrorism and Nonproliferation of the Committee on International Relations, House of Representatives, 109th Congress), March 10, 2005, <http://commdocs.house.gov/committees/intlrel/hfa998 25.000/hfa99825_0f.htm> (February 3, 2009).

11. Centers for Disease Control and Prevention, "Injuries Associated with Landmines and Unexploded Ordnance—Afghanistan, 1997–2002," September 12, 2003, <http://www.cdc.gov/mmwr/preview/mmwrhtml/ mm5236a2.htm> (February 3, 2009).

12. Robert Marquand, "The reclusive ruler who runs the Taliban," *Christian Science Monitor*, October 10, 2001, <http://www.csmonitor.com/2001/1010/p1s4-wosc.html> (February 3, 2009).

13. Molly Moore, "The Taliban's Deadly Rise to Power; From Refugee Camp Radicals to Rulers of Afghanistan, Group Prospered With Pakistan's Patronage," *Washington Post*, September 16, 2001, p. A14.

14. Bergen, p. 99.

15. Ibid., p. 96.

16. Dean E. Murphy and Robin Wright, "Bombs Rock 2 U.S. Embassies; Attacks in Kenya, Tanzania Kill 80, Hurt 1,700; Car blasts in Nairobi, Dar es Salaam occur minutes apart. Eight Americans are among the dead; dozens of people are missing," *Los Angeles Times*, August 8, 1998, p. 1.

17. Judy Aita, "Victims Retell Horrors of Nairobi Embassy Bombing in Court," U.S. Department of State, March 7, 2001, <http://usinfo.state.gov/is/Archive_Index/Victims_Retell_Horrors_of_Nairobi_Embassy_Bombing.html> (September 1, 2007).

18. Judy Aita, "Victims of Tanzanian Bombing Tell of Tragedy," U.S. Department of State, March 14, 2001, <http://usinfo.org/wf-archive/2001/010314/epf304.htm> (April 8, 2009).

19. "Two Attacks Were Not The Work Of Amateurs, State Department Spokesman Says; Embassy Bombings Kill 82; Officials Tighten Security At All U.S. Minstries; The Ones In Kenya And Tanzania Were Considered 'Low Risk'; World Governments Condemn Violence," *Winston-Salem* (N.C.) *Journal*, August 8, 1998, p. 1.

20. Bergen, p. 171.

21. Ibid.

22. "Blast Rips U.S. Ship, 6 Sailors Dead, 11 Missing," *The* (Cleveland) *Plain Dealer*, October 13, 2000, p. 1A.

23. John J. Lumpkin, "'I Felt the Ship Rock,' Sailor Recalls," *Albuquerque Journal*, November 10, 2000, p. A1.

24. National Commission on Terrorist Attacks Upon the United States, p. 153.

25. Ibid., pp. 235–236.

26. "Statement of Jose E. Melendez-Perez to the National Commission on Terrorist Attacks Upon The United States," January 26, 2004, <http://www.9-11commission.gov/hearings/hearing7/witness_melendez.htm> (April 8, 2009).

27. Thomas H. Kean and Lee H. Hamilton, *Without*

Precedent: The Inside Story of the 9/11 Commission (New York: Vintage 2007) p. 137.

Chapter 3 The 9/11 Attack Continues

1. Jim Dwyer and Kevin Flynn, *102 Minutes: The Untold Story of the Fight to Survive Inside the Twin Towers* (New York: Times Books, 2006), p. 64.

2. Thomas H. Kean and Lee H. Hamilton, *Without Precedent: The Inside Story of the 9/11 Commission* (New York: Vintage, 2007), p. 222.

3. *New York Times*, "Accounts From the South Tower," May 26, 2002, <http://www.nytimes.com/2002/05/26/nyregion/26STOWER.html> (February 3, 2009).

4. Ibid.

5. Ibid.

6. Ibid.

7. Ibid.

8. Ibid.

9. Dwyer and Flynn, p. 114.

10. *New York Times*, "Accounts From the South Tower."

11. Ibid.

12. Ibid.

13. Dwyer and Flynn, p. 82.

14. Paul Grondahl, "A father and a hero," *TimesUnion.com*, September 7, 2003, <http://timesunion.com/AspStories/story.asp?storyID=167529&category=FRONTPG&BCCode=SEP11> (February 3, 2009).

15. Dwyer and Flynn, p. 84.

16. Jim Dwyer, "Fresh Glimpse in 9/11 Files of the Struggles

for Survival," *New York Times*, August 29, 2003, <http://www.nytimes.com/2003/08/29/nyregion/ 29WTC.html?ei=5007&en=d6a28710d9bcfd8c&ex=13 77489600&partner=USERLAND&pagewanted=all> (February 3, 2009).

17. Ibid.

18. National Commission on Terrorist Attacks Upon the United States, p. 25.

19. Ibid., p. 9.

20. Ibid., pp. 9–10.

21. Mary Beth Sheridan, "Loud Boom, Then Flames in Hallways; Pentagon Employees Flee Fire, Help Rescue Injured Co-Workers," *Washington Post*, September 12, 2001, p. A15.

22. Robert Schlesinger and Wayne Washington, "After Assault on Pentagon, Orderly Response," *Boston Globe*, September 12, 2001, p. A3.

23. Barbara Vobejda, "Extensive Casualties in Wake of Pentagon Attack," *Washingtonpost.com*, September 11, 2001, <http://www.washingtonpost.com/wp-rv/ metro/daily/sep01/attack.html> (February 3, 2009).

24. Richard T. Cooper, "Outside Pentagon, a Defenseless Feeling ..." *Los Angeles Times*, September 12, 2001, <http://articles.latimes.com/2001/sep/12/news/ mn-44935> (February 3, 2009).

Chapter 4 The Collapse

1. National Commission on Terrorist Attacks Upon the United States, *The 9/11 Commission Report: Final Report of the National Commission on Terrorist Attacks Upon the*

United States, authorized edition (New York: W. W. Norton & Company, 2004), p. 40.

2. National Institute of Standards and Technology, *Final Reports of the Federal Building and Fire Investigation of the World Trade Center Disaster*, Chapter Nine – Appendix C, pp. 79–80, <http://wtc.nist.gov/NCSTAR1/PDF/NCSTAR%201-A%20Chap%209_Appx%20C.pdf> (April 8, 2009).

3. Jim Dwyer and Kevin Flynn, *102 Minutes: The Untold Story of the Fight to Survive Inside the Twin Towers* (New York: Times Books, 2006), p. 203.

4. National Institute of Standards and Technology (NIST) Federal Building and Fire Safety Investigation of the World Trade Center Disaster, *Answers to Frequently Asked Questions*, August 30, 2006, <http://wtc.nist.gov/pubs/factsheets/faqs_8_2006.htm> (February 3, 2009).

5. N. R. Kleinfield, "U.S. Attacked; Hijacked Jets Destroy Twin Towers and Hit Pentagon in Day of Terror," *New York Times*, September 12, 2001, p. A1, <http://query.nytimes.com/gst/fullpage.html?res=9D0CE4DC1238F931A2575AC0A9679C8B63&sec=&spon=&pagewanted=all> (February 3, 2009).

6. Gady A. Epstein, Michael Stroh, and Todd Richissin, "Witnesses come face to face with terror," *Baltimore Sun*, September 12, 2001, p. 7A, <http://cltv.trb.com/news/politics/bal-te.scene12sep12,0,4876119.story> (February 3, 2009).

7. Associated Press, "Witnesses describe scenes of terror in New York City," *Tulsa World*, September 11, 2001, p. 3, <http://www.tulsaworld.com/news/article.aspx?articleID=010911_At_s3witne> (February 3, 2009).

8. Dwyer and Flynn, p. 223.

9. Ibid., p. 235.

10. Kleinfield.

11. Amanda Ripley, "We're under attack," *Time.com*, 2001, <http://www.time.com/time/subscriber/poy2001/poyoral.html> (February 3, 2009).

12. Eric Pooley, "Mayor of the World," *Time.com*, 2001, <http://www.time.com/time/subscriber/poy2001/poyprofile.html> (February 3, 2009).

13. National Commission on Terrorist Attacks Upon the United States, p. 11.

14. Ibid., p. 12

15. Kim Barker, Louise Kiernan, and Steve Mills, "Heroes stand up even in the hour of their deaths," *Chicago Tribune*, September 30, 2001, p. 1.

16. Ibid.

17. Ibid.

18. National Commission on Terrorist Attacks Upon the United States, pp. 13–14.

19. Stephen Braun and Aaron Zitner, "On United Flight 93, a Call for Help," *Los Angeles Times*, September 12, 2001, p. A23, <http://articles.latimes.com/2001/sep/12/news/mn-44942> (February 3, 2009).

20. National Commission on Terrorist Attacks Upon the United States, p. 14.

Chapter 5 Aftermath

1. Jim Dwyer, "A Nation Challenged: Objects; Beneath the Rubble, the Only Tool Was a Pair of Cuffs," *New York Times*, October 30, 2001, p. B1, <http://query.nytimes.com/

gst/fullpage.html?res=9E00E5D81430F933A05753C1A9
679C8B63&sec=&spon=&pagewanted=all> (February 3,
2009).

2. Ibid.

3. Jim Nolan and Nicole Weisensee Egan, "Under the rubble, two cops learn about life; Miraculous series of coincidences rescued them from WTC," *Philadelphia Daily News*, December 31, 2001, p. 7.

4. Ibid.

5. Rebecca Leung, "Last Man Out: Sgt. John McLoughlin Describes His Rescue From Ground Zero After 9/11," *CBS News*, November 24, 2004, <http://www.cbsnews.com/stories/2004/11/23/60II/main657404.shtml> (April 9, 2009).

6. Michael Grunwald, "Up Close at Ground Zero, Desolation and Dust," *Washington Post*, September 21, 2001, p. A20.

7. Susan Sachs, "A Delicate Removal of Debris, With Monstrous Machines and Gloved Hands," *New York Times*, September 14, 2001, p. A10.

8. Ibid.

9. Bill Dries and Lela Garlington, "'Carnage At Its Worst' Found at Pentagon," *The* (Memphis, Tenn.) *Commercial Appeal*, September 17, 2001, p. A4.

10. "President Freezes Terrorists' Assets, Remarks by the President, Secretary of the Treasury O'Neill and Secretary of State Powell on Executive Order," The White House, September 12, 2001, <http://georgewbush-whitehouse.archives.gov/news/releases/2001/09/images/20010924-4.html> (April 5, 2009).

11. *Public Law 107-39, 107th Congress, Joint Resolution*, U.S. Government Printing Office, September 18, 2001, <http://frwebgate.access.gpo.gov/cgi-bin/ getdoc.cgi?dbname=107_cong_public_laws&docid= f:publ039.107> (February 3, 2009).

12. *Public Law 107-40, 107th Congress, Joint Resolution*, U.S. Government Printing Office, September 18, 2001, <http://frwebgate.access.gpo.gov/cgi-bin/ getdoc.cgi?dbname=107_cong_public_laws&docid=f:pu bl040.107> (February 3, 2009).

13. "NATO and the Scourge of Terrorism: What Is Article 5?" North Atlantic Treaty Organization, February 18, 2005, <http://www.nato.int/terrorism/five.htm> (February 3, 2009).

14. Walter Hamilton, "Markets Get Ready to Reopen," *Los Angeles Times*, September 16, 2001, p. A3.

15. Greg Schneider and Carol Vinzant, "Stocks Continue to Fall; Dow Off 13% in 4 Days; Indexes at Lowest Level in More Than 2 Years," *Washington Post*, September 21, 2001, p. A01.

16. "Airline, other travel stocks take dives," *Advocate* (Baton Rouge, La.), September 18, 2001, p. 6A.

17. Hanna Rosin and John Mintz, "Muslim Leaders Struggle With Mixed Messages," *Washington Post*, October 2, 2001, p. A16.

18. "'Islam is Peace' Says President: Remarks by the President at Islamic Center of Washington, D.C.," The White House, September 17, 2001, <http:// georgewbush-whitehouse.archives.gov/news/releases/ 2001/09/20010917-11.html> (April 5, 2009).

19. Richard Winton, "Hate Crimes Soar Following Attacks," *Los Angeles Times*, December 21, 2001, p. B1.

20. Charles M. Madigan, "Get bin Laden 'dead or alive,' Bush says," *Chicago Tribune*, September 17, 2001, p. 1.

21. T. R. Reid, "Blair: 'No Compromise'; Taliban Is Warned," *Washington Post*, October 3, 2001, p. A12.

Chapter 6 Getting Answers

1. Lev Grossman, "Why the 9/11 Conspiracy Theories Won't Go Away," *Time*, September 3, 2006, <http://www.time.com/time/magazine/article/0,9171,1531304-1,00.html> (February 3, 2009).

2. National Institute of Standards and Technology, *Final Report on the Collapse of the World Trade Center Towers*, September 2005, <http://wtc.nist.gov/NCSTAR1/PDF/NCSTAR%201.pdf> (April 5, 2009).

3. "Debunking the 9/11 Myths: Special Report," *Popular Mechanics*, March 2005, <http://www.popularmechanics.com/technology/military_law/1227842.html> (February 3, 2009).

4. Peter Tyson, "Towers of Innovation," *NOVA online*, August 2006, <http://www.pbs.org/wgbh/nova/wtc/innovation.html> (February 3, 2009).

5. "Impact to Collapse," *NOVA online*, August 2006, <http://www.pbs.org/wgbh/nova/wtc/sunder.html> (February 3, 2009).

6. Ibid.

7. Ibid.

8. Ibid.

9. Jim Dwyer and Ford Fessenden, "One Hotel's Fight to

the Finish; At the Marriott, a Portal to Safety as the Towers Fell," *New York Times*, September 11, 2002, p. B1.

10. "Debunking the 9/11 Myths: Special Report."

11. Thomas H. Kean and Lee H. Hamilton, *Without Precedent: The Inside Story of the 9/11 Commission* (New York: Vintage, 2007), p. 14.

12. "Statement of Harry Waizer to the National Commission on Terrorist Attacks Upon the United States," March 31, 2003, <http://www.9-11commission.gov/hearings/hearing1/witness_waizer.htm> (February 3, 2009).

13. Ibid.

14. "Statement of Stephen Push to the National Commission on Terrorist Attacks Upon the United States," March 31, 2003, <http://www.9-1commission.gov/hearings/hearing1/witness_push.htm> (February 3, 2009).

15. Kean and Hamilton, p. 324.

16. "Impact to Collapse."

17. National Commission on Terrorist Attacks Upon the United States, *The 9/11 Commission Report: Final Report of the National Commission on Terrorist Attacks Upon the United States: Executive Summary*, n.d., <http://www.9-11commission.gov/report/911Report_Exec.pdf> (February 3, 2009).

18. Ibid.

Chapter 7 Moving Forward, Remembering, and Healing

1. "The Odds of Dying from ...," National Security

Council, 2005, <http://www.nsc.org/research/odds.aspx> (April 5, 2009).

2. Benjamin Friedman, "Think Again: Homeland Security," *Foreign Policy*, July/August 2005, <http://www.foreignpolicy.com/story/cms.php?story_id= 3079> (February 3, 2009).

3. "The Odds of Dying from . . . ."

4. Friedman.

5. Bill Bush, "Terrorism Rates Pretty Low On List Of Threats; Driving, other daily actions much riskier, statistics indicate," *Columbus* (Ohio) *Dispatch*, December 23, 2003, p. 01A.

6. Mary Louise Kelly, "In 2006, Attacks Were Thwarted. But Why?" *All Things Considered*, National Public Radio, December 26, 2006, <http://www.npr.org/templates/ story/story.php?storyId=6682409> (February 3, 2009).

7. Daniel Byman, interview with author, August 2007.

8. Ibid.

9. U.S. Department of State, *Patterns of Global Terrorism 2003*, April 2004, p. xi, <http://www.state.gov/ documents/organization/31912.pdf> (February 3, 2009).

10. Byman.

11. Mark Mazzetti, "Spy Agencies Say Iraq War Worsens Terrorism Threat," *New York Times*, September 24, 2006, p. 1.1.

12. Kean and Hamilton, pp. 342–346.

13. "9/11 Five Years Later: Successes and Challenges," The White House, September 2006, <http://georgewbush-whitehouse.archives.gov/nsc/waronterror/2006> (April 5, 2009).

14. Byman.

15. "FDNY Memorial Wall, a Gift from Holland & Knight, Honors Members of the New York City Fire Department and Holland & Knight Partner Who Perished on 9-11-2001," FDNY Memorial Wall, n.d., <http://www.fdnytenhouse.com/fdnywall/index.htm> (February 3, 2009).

16. David W. Dunlap, "Stairs to Remain Intact in Ground Zero Plan," *New York Times*, August 6, 2007, p. B3.

17. "Freedom Tower Cornerstone Laid at New York Ceremony," National Public Radio, July 4, 2004, <http://www.npr.org/templates/story/story.php?storyId=3129012> (February 3, 2009).

18. Kevin Coyne, "Remembering, From a Distance," *New York Times*, September 10, 2006, p. 14NJ.1.

Glossary

barbarism—A cruel or uncivilized nature.

bipartisan—Involving two political parties.

burqa—A garment with veiled eyeholes that covers a woman from head to toe.

cantilevered—Having a projecting structure supported or attached only at one end.

Communism—A political system that gives ownership and control of wealth to the state.

decadence—Decay in society's moral values.

diplomacy—International relations and communication between countries.

evacuate—To leave a place.

extremist—Someone who advocates or supports extreme measures.

fatwa—A formal religious decree issued by an Islamic leader.

infrastructure—Large-scale public systems, services, and facilities.

jihad—Literally, "struggle"; often used to refer to a holy war against peoples, organizations, or countries regarded as hostile to Islam.

martyr—Someone who chooses to die for a strongly held (often religious) belief.

triage—The process of prioritizing people for medical treatment.

ultimatum—A demand that includes a threat if the demand is not met.

Further Reading

Anderson, Dale. *The Terrorist Attacks of September 11, 2001.* Milwaukee: World Almanac Library, 2004.

Burns, Vincent, and Kate Dempsey Peterson. *Terrorism: A Documentary and Reference Guide.* Westport, Conn.: Greenwood Press, 2005.

Frank, Mitch. *Understanding September 11th: Answering Questions About the Attacks on America.* New York: Viking, 2002.

Hampton, Wilborn. *September 11, 2001: Attack on New York City: Interviews and Accounts.* London: Walker, 2003.

The New York Times. *A Nation Challenged: A Visual History of 9/11 and Its Aftermath.* New York: Scholastic Nonfiction, 2002.

Thoms, Annie, editor. *With Their Eyes: September 11th: The View From a High School.* New York: HarperTempest, 2002.

Internet Addresses

Inside 9/11: National Geographic Channel
**<http://channel.nationalgeographic.com/series/
inside-911>**

The 9/11 Records: *The New York Times*
**<http://www.nytimes.com/indexes/2005/11/30/
nyregion/nyregionspecial3/index.html>**

Nova: Building on Ground Zero
<http://www.pbs.org/wgbh/nova/wtc/>

Index